The Beaver Book of Lists

A short list of things about this book
1 It consists of lists
2 Some of them are funny
3 Some of them are factual
4 They're all about children's things
5 Except for the ones not about children's things
6 But they're all meant to be of interest to all children

An even shorter list of things about Hunter Davies:
1 He's the editor of this book
2 He edited the *Book of British Lists* which you must have heard about as it was a best-seller and terribly good
3 He is very fond of stamps, quite fond of railways and terribly fond of lists
4 He has three children and writes a column about them every week in *Punch* called 'Father's Day'

The Beaver Book of
LISTS

Hunter Davies

Illustrated by Graham Thompson

Beaver Books

First published in 1981 by
The Hamlyn Publishing Group Limited
London · New York · Sydney · Toronto
Astronaut House, Feltham, Middlesex, England
Paperback Division: Hamlyn Paperbacks,
Banda House, Cambridge Grove,
Hammersmith, London W6 0LE
Reprinted 1981

© Copyright Text Inter-Action Trust Limited 1981
© Copyright Illustrations
The Hamlyn Publishing Group Limited 1981
ISBN 0 600 20394 8

Typeset, printed and bound in Great Britain by
Hazell Watson & Viney Limited, Aylesbury, Bucks
Set in Garamond

Contents

Acknowledgements

In addition to the staff and pupils of the schools mentioned in the Introduction, and the people and organisations credited in particular lists, the author and publishers would like to thank Sandy Ransford, for her assistance in compiling the book; Margaret Histed, for her painstaking research; and Peter Watson, for his lists.

Introduction

Yes, but what sort of lists are they? Well, just lists, really. What more can I say? Turn over a few pages, if you haven't done so already, and you'll see some of them. Lists of facts and figures, biggests and smallests, records and achievements, places and people, opinions and trends, the most loved and the most hated.

Amaze your friends by reading out to them some of the dafter pieces of information. Be amazed yourself when you totally disagree with some of the opinions listed. 'That is certainly not *my* favourite school dinner. . . .'

The common denominator is children. We've either based the lists on the opinions of children or have chosen the lists because we think, or hope, that they will be of particular interest to children and young people.

One of the main sources of information has been a survey we carried out of roughly 600 children, aged from six to twelve years of age, in selected schools round Great Britain. We sent out a leaflet containing twenty questions, ranging from what is your favourite TV programme, football player, pop star or joke to how much pocket money do you get and what do you want to be when you grow up. We analysed the answers, using all the latest modern devices, and both sets of fingers, and the results are inside. They provide fascinating reading.

We are naturally very grateful to the staff and pupils of all the schools who helped. They will be getting free copies of the book. So it was worthwhile, after all. The schools were, in alphabetical order,

Claremont Fan Court School, Esher, Surrey
Comberton Middle School, Kidderminster, Worcs
Fairstead C. P. School, King's Lynn, Norfolk
Filton High School, Stoke Gifford, Bristol
Kirkintilloch High School, Kirkintilloch, Glasgow
Langley Park School for Boys, Beckenham, Kent
Outward Grange Comprehensive School, Wakefield, Yorks
Pott Row First School, Grimston, King's Lynn, Norfolk
Strand-on-the-Green Infant School, Chiswick, London
Strand-on-the-Green Junior School, Chiswick, London

In the book, we have referred to it as the Beaver Survey so you will know where the information has come from. The other lists have been assembled by our own researchers or taken from Government publications or reference books. A few have come from the *Book of British Lists*, which I did last year, bringing them up to date where necessary.

If *you* have any lists, which you think might be of interest to other children, please send them in and we might be able to use them in a future edition of this book.

It's called the *Beaver Book of Lists* because in May, 1981, Beaver Books are celebrating their fifth birthday as publishers of paperback books for children. Happy birthday, Beaver. They wanted to do something special, and something specially for children. We all hope you enjoy it.

Hunter Davies,
London, January, 1981

1 School

And the common denominator amongst all children is school, so what better, or worse, way to begin. We start with a few opinions about school and then move on, quickly, to some famous schools and colleges.

Teachers

Beaver survey

In our school questionnaire, we asked children their favourite slang word for teacher. There were a few general names – 'beak', 'teach', 'the boss'; and several unprintable ones, of which 'creeps' and 'Hitler' were about the most polite. Here's a list of the most original. If any teacher recognises him- or herself, it wasn't really you, honest. . . .

Granny Boy O	The Walking Mop
Tadpole	Oakee Shoe
Mrs Headless	Key

Percy Penguin   Puffing Billy
Ronald's Speak   Turnip
Red Dragon   Macaroni
Margery Mole

Best school subject

Beaver survey

1 maths
2 PE and games
3 English
4 art, or art and craft
5 history
6 reading
7 needlework, metalwork and woodwork
8 drama, French, geography, cooking and home economics
9 technical studies
10 humanities

Maths was only slightly more popular than PE and games. In the bottom half of the list, the subjects were almost equal in popularity.

Worst subject at school

Beaver survey

1 maths
2 English
3 French
4 music and RE
5 science
6 geography
7 humanities and handwriting
8 art
9 diary writing
10 history, and PE and games

So maths was the most liked and also the most disliked subject, which comes of asking two different questions. Although it topped both lists, it was only marginally the most liked subject whereas on the most disliked list, it was clearly the leader. Children obviously clearly divide on their feelings about maths, though perhaps the way different teachers present the subject has an effect on its popularity.

Smallest primary school classes

These are the local education authorities in England and Wales where the pupil-teacher ratio is under 20 to 1. So if you want to be in a small class, you know where to move.

Inner London	15·1
Dyfed	17·3
Powys	17·7
Brent	17·7
Haringey	18·2
Newham	18·5
Wolverhampton	19·1
Ealing	19·2
Newcastle	19·8
Manchester	19·9
Gwynedd	19·9

Largest primary school classes

Tameside	24·0
Bromley	24·1
Bolton	24·1
Hampshire	24·2
Bexley	24·4
Somerset	24·5
Oxfordshire	24·6
Hereford & Worcester	24·6
Wirral	24·7

Avon	24·7
Dudley	25·7
Stockport	26·7

Top schools: Oxbridge Awards 1979–80

These are the schools which got the most open awards, scholarships or exhibitions to Oxford and Cambridge during the 1979–80 academic year. The first two columns, which list the number of boys or girls post O-levels (roughly, the sixth form) gives an idea of the size of each school. Manchester Grammar School, which got the most awards the previous year (33) dropped to fifth place this year. Eton, second in 1978–79 (28) came top. Eton is of course a very big school. Proportionally, King Edward's, Birmingham, and Westminster both did better, as did some others.

school	pupils post O-level boys	girls	awards
Eton College	644	—	36
St Paul's	406	—	27
Dulwich College	471	3	26
Haberdashers' Aske's School, Elstree	349	—	26
Manchester Grammar School	537	—	24
King Edward's, Birmingham	223	—	20
Westminster	226	75	20
Bradford Grammar S.	373	—	17
Marlborough College	394	101	16
Winchester College	407	—	16
Nottingham High S.	235	—	15
St Paul's Girls' S.	—	207	15
Newcastle Royal Grammar S.	270	—	14
Charterhouse	352	46	13
St Alban's	227	—	13
Birkenhead	226	—	12
Cheltenham Ladies' College	—	291	12

City of London	254	—	11
King's College School, Wimbledon	258	—	11
Leeds Grammar School	293	—	11
Sevenoaks	308	70	11
Trinity School, Croydon	222	—	11
Abingdon	240	—	10
Ampleforth College	272	—	10
King Edward VI, Southampton	245	—	10
King's School, Canterbury	315	70	10
Rugby	355	41	10
Aylesbury Grammar S.	280	—	9
High Wycombe Royal G. S.	376	—	9
Malvern College	262	1	9
University Coll. S., Hampstead	220	—	9
Warwick	108	—	9
Wellington College	328	42	9
Brentwood	287	17	8
Clifton College	306	—	8
Desborough S., Maidenhead	159	—	8
Dr Challoner's G. S., Amersham	316	—	8
Lancaster Royal G. S.	234	—	8
Loughborough G. S.	221	—	8
Shrewsbury	255	—	8
Bedales S., Petersfield	86	83	7
Bolton (Boys' Division)	231	—	7
Bryanston	155	79	7
Harrow	321	3	7
Leys S., Cambridge	170	—	7
Reading	158	—	7
Solihull	202	52	7
Birkenhead H. S.	—	178	6
Bristol G. S.	293	37	6
Coventry	439	50	6
Cranleigh	220	45	6
Eltham College	124	9	6
Hymers College, Hull	162	12	6
Kingswood S., Bath	125	62	6
King's S., Worcester	199	39	6
Merchant Taylors' S., Northwood	220	—	6

Oxford High School	—	150	6
Radley College	280	—	6
Rossall School, Fleetwood	167	5	6
St Benedict's School, Ealing	170	14	6
Stonyhurst College	204	—	6
Varndean 6th Form Coll., Brighton	160	135	6
Whitgift School, Croydon	227	—	6
William Ellis	189	—	6

Top quiz schools

Top of the Form is BBC Radio's long-established, annual general knowledge competition for teams of secondary school children throughout the country. The teams are each made up of four members with ages ranging from eleven to eighteen. These schools have been the winners:

Top of the Form

1948   Royal High School, Edinburgh
1949   Elgin Academy, Scotland
1950   Robert Gordon's College, Aberdeen
1951   Morgan Academy, Dundee
1952   Bangor Grammar School, North Wales
1953   Nicholson Institute, Stornoway
1954   Grove Park School, Wrexham
1955   Newtown Girls' County Grammar School, Wales
1956   Sutton Coldfield High School
1957   Wycombe High School for Girls, High Wycombe
1958   Gordon Schools, Huntly, Aberdeenshire
1959   Mackie Academy, Stonehaven, Kincardine
1960   Grove Park Grammar School for Girls, Wrexham
1961   Archbishop Holgate's Grammar School, York
1962   Hull Grammar School
1963   Cambridgeshire High School for Boys, Cambridge
1964   The Academy, Montrose
1965   The High School, Falkirk
1966   St Martin-in-the-Fields High School, London

1967	Greenock Academy
1968	Grove Park School, Wrexham
1969	Queen Elizabeth Grammar School for Girls, Carmarthen
1970	Wyggeston Boys' School, Leicester
1971	Cheadle Hulme School, Cheadle, Cheshire
1972	The County Girls' Grammar School, Newbury
1973	Kirkcudbright Academy, Scotland
1974	The Grammar School, Cheltenham
1975	King William's College, Isle of Man
1976	County High School for Girls, Macclesfield
1977	Wellington School, Somerset
1978	Brinkburn School, Hartlepool
1979	Chislehurst & Sidcup Grammar School, Greater London
1980	Wycombe High School for Girls, High Wycombe

University Challenge

Since 1964, Granada Television has organised the competition between teams from British universities. Here are the winners:

1964	Leicester University
1965	New College, Oxford
1966	Oriel College, Oxford
1967	University of Sussex
1968	Keble College, Oxford
1969	University of Sussex
1970	Churchill College, Cambridge
1971	Sidney Sussex College, Cambridge
1972	University College, Oxford
1973	Fitzwilliam College, Cambridge
1974	Trinity College, Cambridge
1975	Keble College, Oxford
1976	University College, Oxford
1977	University of Durham
1978	Sidney Sussex College, Cambridge
1979	*University Challenge* was not completed because of the ITV disruption
1980	Merton College, Oxford

Intelligence

There is no foolproof way of measuring intelligence, not even IQ tests, but graduating from a university must prove something. Here are the areas of England inhabited by arguably the most intelligent people. It is based on local education authority reports published by the Department of Education.

Highest percentage of the population with university degrees, 1978

1	Richmond upon Thames	16·5
2	Surrey (as a whole)	14·8
3	Bromley	13·4
4	Barnet	13·3
5	Stockport	12·7
6	Buckinghamshire	12·4
7	Kingston upon Thames	12·4
8	Harrow	12·0
9	Sutton	11·6
10	Oxfordshire	11·5

Lowest percentage of the population with university degrees, 1978

1	Barking	2·0
2	Newham	2·5
3	Sandwell	3·0
4	Knowsley	3·5
5	Tameside	4·8
6	Oldham	5·3
7	Manchester	5·6
8	Walsall	5·8
9	Gateshead	5·8
10	Wigan	5·9

Universities

British universities in order of age

When you leave school, you might consider one of these as a way of putting in three or four years. They are the universities in England, Scotland and Northern Ireland. The dates refer to their founding as separate universities – though several were founded as colleges before that date. The colleges of the University of Wales are listed separately.

	no. of students
Oxford, 1249	8 781
Cambridge, 1284	9 378
St Andrews, 1411	3 451
Glasgow, 1451	10 515
Aberdeen, 1495	4 816
Edinburgh, 1583	11 250
Durham, 1832	4 211
London, 1836	46 438
Manchester, 1851	15 009
Newcastle, 1852*	7 463
Birmingham, 1880	8 476
Liverpool, 1903	8 138
Leeds, 1904	9 822
Sheffield, 1905	7 432
Queens, Belfast, 1908	5 816
Bristol, 1909	6 006
Reading, 1926	5 990
Nottingham, 1948	5 797
Southampton, 1952	5 988
Hull, 1954	5 134
Exeter, 1955	5 045
Leicester, 1957	4 226
Sussex, 1961	4 575
Keele, 1962	2 805
East Anglia (Norwich), 1963	4 061

* Originally part of Durham University.

York, 1963	2 650
Strathclyde, 1964	6 402
Lancaster, 1964	4 196
Essex, 1964	2 786
Ulster, 1965	1 570
Warwick, 1965	5 099
Kent (Canterbury), 1965	3 747
Heriot-Watt, 1966	3 132
Loughborough, 1966	5 760
Aston (Birmingham), 1966	5 711
The City University, 1966	3 224
Brunel, 1966	4 450
Bath, 1966	3 017
Bradford, 1966	4 250
Surrey, 1966	2 839
Dundee, 1967	2 911
Stirling, 1967	2 471
Salford, 1967	4 014

University of Wales, 1893

	no. of students
Aberystwyth	2 633
Bangor	2 452
Cardiff, Institute of Science and Technology	2 457
Cardiff, National School of Medicine	661
Cardiff, University College	4 284
Lampeter	643
Swansea	3 116

University courses, UK, 1975–6

Courses taken by full-time undergraduates:

1	Social, administrative and business studies	23·5
2	Science	23·0
3	Engineering and technology	13·8
4	Language, literature and area studies	12·8
5	Medicine, dentistry and health	11·9
6	Arts other than languages	10·3
7	Agriculture, forestry and veterinary science	1·9
8	Architecture and other professional and vocational subjects	1·8
9	Education	1·0

2 Food

Food, glorious food, there's nothing quite like it when you're feeling rude. Please do not make a mess over these lists of favourite foods or drop anything over them. Other people might want to read them after you....

We've digested some more figures from our survey and here are the most liked and most disliked meals.

Most hated school dinner (main course)

Beaver survey

1 salad
2 fish or fish fingers
3 cheese pie or egg and cheese pie
4 stew, with or without dumplings
5 liver
6 sausages, with or without chips or beans
7 ravioli

8 mince or mince pie
  9 pork pie
 10 ham- or beefburgers

Lots of food-haters also said they hated vegetables, especially potatoes, cabbage and mushy peas. They would, wouldn't they. . . .

Most hated pudding

Beaver survey

  1 rice
  2 semolina
  3 sponge (other than chocolate)
  4 apple pie or crumble or baked apples
  5 rhubarb or rhubarb pie
  6 chocolate pudding with chocolate sauce
  7 bananas and custard
  8 cake, especially ginger cake
  9 prunes, currant roly-poly, and blancmange
 10 tapioca

Custard is disliked by a lot of children, but a lot said they really liked it. Custard would give no comment when asked for its opinion on children. Cowardy custard. . . .

Favourite school dinner (main course)

Beaver survey

  1 fish and chips or fish fingers and chips (often with beans)
  2 roast meat (beef is the favourite)
  3 sausage and chips (often with beans)
  4 ham- or beefburgers (usually with chips and beans)
  5 chicken, including chicken pie and sweet and sour chicken
  6 salad, and shepherd's pie
  7 mutton pie (Scotland only)

8 pasta, i.e. spaghetti, macaroni cheese, and hot dogs
9 mince, with potatoes or chips
10 pie and chips

Dishes with chips and/or beans were very popular, and mutton pie was very popular in Scotland.

Favourite pudding

Beaver survey

1 ice-cream
2 cake, including sponge cake, chocolate cake, shortbread, etc.
3 apple pie or crumble
4 yogurt
5 jelly, or jelly and cream
6 chocolate pudding and jam roll/pie/sponge
7 treacle pudding and rice pudding
8 semolina, with or without jam
9 lemon meringue pie or meringues
10 rhubarb crumble

Custard has asked us to point out that though technically not a pudding, within the meaning of the Pudding Act, it is also popular in many, many schools. So there.

And, for the sake of comparison, this is what the professionals found out about children's favourite meals. A survey carried out by Carrick James Market Research for Wall's Ice-Cream Limited came up with the following:

Main course

1 fish and chips	13 per cent
2 roast chicken	8 per cent
3 roast (unspecified)	7 per cent
4 roast beef and Yorkshire pudding	7 per cent

5	steak and chips	7 per cent
6	curry	4 per cent
7	chips	4 per cent
8	salad*	4 per cent

(more popular with girls than boys in the older age groups)

9	steak and kidney pie	3 per cent
10	beefburger and chips	3 per cent
11	fish fingers and chips	3 per cent
12	sausage and chips	2 per cent
13	spaghetti bolognese	3 per cent
14	others	30 per cent
	don't know	2 per cent

Pudding

1	ice-cream	15 per cent
2	apple pie/crumble	14 per cent
3	other pies/tarts/flans	11 per cent
4	sponge puddings	11 per cent
5	milk puddings including rice	8 per cent
6	fruit excluding strawberries	6 per cent
7	trifle	3 per cent
8	strawberries and cream	2 per cent
9	yogurt	2 per cent
10	others	24 per cent
	don't know	4 per cent

Favourite sweets

Beaver survey

Children's favourite sweets were difficult to sort out because some gave types of sweets and some gave actual brand names. So we divided the sweets into categories.

1 chocolate and chocolate bars (Mars Bars were the favourite chocolate bar)
2 toffees (chocolate toffees were favourite)
3 sherbet and fizzy sweets

4 mints (especially Polos and Extra Strong) and bon-bons
 5 gums, especially wine gums
 6 bubble gum
 7 cola sweets
 8 humbugs
 9 liquorice
10 chews (which are really types of toffee)
11 jelly sweets (Jelly Tots are small children's favourites)

Rowntree/Mackintosh report that a 1979 survey among children up to fifteen revealed the following top six favourite sweets:

1 Kit Kat
2 Smarties
3 Fruit Pastilles
4 Quality Street chocolate assortment
5 Yorkie
6 Rolo

And Cadbury's say that the top five of their brands most frequently bought by children aged five to thirteen are:

1 Crunchie
2 Flake
3 Fudge
4 Dairy Milk
5 Double Decker

Favourite ice-cream flavour

Beaver survey

1 chocolate
2 strawberry
3 vanilla
4 mint choc chip
5 mint
6 raspberry/raspberry ripple

7 orange
  8 rum and raisin
  9 coffee
10 lime

Chocolate and strawberry were way ahead of the other flavours. Young children seemed to prefer strawberry; flavours such as rum and raisin were more appreciated by older children.

Favourite ice-lolly flavour

Beaver survey

  1 orange
  2 strawberry
  3 cola
  4 cider
  5 chocolate
  6 raspberry
  7 banana
  8 lemonade
  9 blackcurrant
10 lime

Ice-cream experts

Having heard from the consumers, here's what spokesmen from some of the big producers say are the favourites.

Wall's report that orange, strawberry and chocolate ice-creams and lollies sell best. Children, they say, like complexity of flavour and shape in lollies – such as their new product Funny Feet, shaped like a foot. Cornetto is very popular with the under-sixteens, and it has been found that they actually buy this product with their own pocket money, rather than asking for money to buy it, or at least 40 per cent of them do.

Lyons say that orange, strawberry and chocolate are the favourite lolly flavours; strawberry, chocolate and vanilla the favourite ice-creams. They say that children prefer a variety of shapes and flavours, such as their Mr Men lollies, which are mixed fruit flavour. Zoom – a mixture of blackberry, strawberry and raspberry flavours – is also popular.

Creamery Fare, which make continental ice-cream, report that their most popular lolly flavours are strawberry, raspberry, lime and cider. Favourite ordinary ice-cream flavours are strawberry, chocolate and coffee; and favourite continental ice-cream flavours are pistachio almond, maple walnut and melon.

Breakfast cereals

The top ten cereals in Britain, 1980

1 Kellogg's Corn Flakes
2 Weetabix
3 Kellogg's All-Bran
4 Nabisco Shredded Wheat
5 Lyons' Ready Brek
6 Kellogg's Rice Krispies
7 Kellogg's Frosties
8 Quaker Sugar Puffs
9 Alpen (Weetabix Ltd)
10 Kellogg's 30% Bran Flakes

Kellogg's, the leading producer, turn out nearly $1\frac{1}{2}$ million packets of cereal every day. If the packed cartons were laid end to end, a day's output would reach from their Manchester plant to Dover, over 250 miles away. The cereal cartons used at Kellogg's account for 25 000 tons of board per year.

Chocolates

In a recent survey carried out by Cadbury's they analysed the popularity of their milk and plain chocolate centres – trying to discover which centres in a box were eaten first.

Cadbury's most popular chocolate centres

1 Hazel Whirl – milk chocolate
2 Noisette Whirl – milk chocolate
3 Caramel – milk or plain chocolate
4 Whole Brazil dipped in plain chocolate

The following six centres are also very popular, but are in no particular order of preference.

1 Hazelnut in soft toffee – milk chocolate
2 Coffee Creme – milk or plain chocolate
3 Hazel Cluster – plain chocolate
4 Fudge – milk or plain chocolate
5 Montelimar – plain chocolate
6 Cherry Creme – plain chocolate

As a general rule, hard, nutty centres are more popular than soft, gooey centres.

Crisps

Britain is a big crisp-munching nation: forty packs of crisps for every man, woman and child are eaten each year. The largest consumers of crisps are the Americans, but we run a close second in an international list of seven.

A spokesman for Smiths' Crisps says: 'Constant research is being carried out to find new flavours that people will want. We recently tried curried crisps but the public didn't take to them at all. Five years ago we re-introduced the old plain crisps with the little blue pack of salt (Salt 'n' Shake) and these are immensely popular. So are square crisps, made from reconstituted potato.'

The ten most popular flavours of crisps in Britain

1 Ready Salted
2 Cheese & Onion
3 Salt & Vinegar
4 Salt 'n' Shake
5 Bovril
6 Beef
7 Smoky Bacon
8 Gammon
9 Chicken
10 Tomato Sauce

The ten most popular proprietary savoury snacks

1 Monster Munch
2 Quavers
3 Country Crunch
4 Outer Spacers
5 Wotsits
6 Frazzles
7 Football Crazy
8 Chipsticks
9 Horror Bags
10 Hula Hoops

Fish

Britain's fishing fleet

Where do fish fingers come from, Daddy? From fish. Where does all the fish come from? Fishing boats. Look, just read all these figures and keep quiet.

The total number of vessels at 31 December 1976 was 9059. This consisted of 6443 in England and Wales and 2616 in Scotland.

Total landed weight (thousand tonnes)   917
Cod   211

Haddock	128
Herring	85
Shellfish	78
Saithe (coalfish)	40
Plaice	32
Other	343

3 Hobbies & Activities

After all that food, you definitely need to get out into the playground and get some fresh air. Or you can take your mind off your tum by sticking in a few stamps.

Favourite playground game or activity

Beaver survey

In our survey, we asked a number of schoolchildren to name their favourite playground occupation.

1 tig (including tunnel tig, aeroplane tig, off-ground tig and chain tig)
2 football
3 ball games other than football or cricket
4 bulldog (or British bulldog)
5 it
6 apparatus games (ropes, wall bars, etc.)
7 talking

8 one man hunt and hide and seek
9 cricket and running
10 cops and robbers

Favourite hobbies

Beaver survey

1 collecting (other than stamps)
2 swimming
3 stamp collecting
4 reading
5 football
6 model-making, especially aeroplanes
7 ball games other than football, and riding
8 cycling
9 fishing
10 sewing, knitting and other crafts

Stamps

Stamp collecting is the world's most popular collecting hobby, and certainly the most popular among the children who helped us with our survey.* (Of all the world's hobbies, it is generally ranked as number two after photography.) There are two million serious stamp collectors in Britain.

These 1980 lists have been provided by Stanley Gibbons, London, the largest international stamp dealers in the world. During 1979 they created a world record for a stamp collection when they paid (US) \$10 million, £5 million, for the Marc Hass collection of early United States postal covers.

---

* It was the most popular single form of collecting, but collecting generally covered so many different items that numerically it came out top in our list.

The top ten British stamps

December 1980
values

1 1902–4 King Edward VII 6d, dull purple, Inland Revenue overprint	£50 000 unused £30 000 used
2 1882 Queen Victoria £1, brown-lilac (watermark large anchor)	£30 000 unused £2000 used
3 1864–79 Queen Victoria 1d, red, plate 77	£30 000 unused £18 000 used
4 1878 Queen Victoria £1, brown-lilac, (watermark Maltese cross)	£25 000 unused £1300 used
5 1902–4 King Edward VII 1/-, green and red, Board of Education overprint	£23 000 unused £10 000 used
6 1883 Queen Victoria 10/-, grey (watermark large anchor)	£22 000 unused £1100 used
7 1887 Queen Victoria 10/-, grey (watermark Maltese cross)	£20 000 unused £900 used
1888 Queen Victoria £1, brown-lilac, Inland Revenue overprint (watermark three crowns)	£19 000 unused £1300 used
8 1890 Queen Victoria £1, brown-lilac Inland Revenue overprint (watermark three crowns)	£18 000 unused £3000 used
9 1902 King Edward VII 10/-, blue, Inland Revenue overprint	£17 000 unused £9500 used

10	1890 Queen Victoria £1, brown-lilac, Inland Revenue overprint (watermark three orbs)	£15 000 unused £2750 used
	1902 King Edward VII £1, green, Inland Revenue overprint	£15 000 unused £3250 used

Notice that a Penny Black, Britain's best-known stamp, is not in the list. Although it was the first postage stamp in the world in 1840, 69 million were printed. However, according to Stanley Gibbons, a Penny Black in good condition is worth around £2500, and a Tuppenny Blue £5500. (Prices at December 1980 for unused stamps.)

The top ten world stamps

		December 1980 values
1	British Guiana 1 cent, black on magenta of 1856	£425 000 unused
2	Mauritius 'Post Office' penny red of 1847	£375 000 unused
3	Mauritius 'Post Office' tuppeny blue of 1847	£240 000 unused
4	Bermuda red 'Penny Perot' 1854	£100 000 unused
	Bermuda red 'Penny Perot' 1856	£100 000 unused
5	Hawaii missionary 2 cents blue of 1851 (approx.	$230 000 used £100 000)
6	British Guiana 2 cents rose 'Cotton Reel' 1851	£55 000 used
7	Great Britain 1902 sixpenny purple, Inland Revenue overprint	£50 000 unused
8	Ceylon fourpenny dull rose of 1857	£45 000 unused
9	Canada 12d black of 1851	£42 000 unused
10	Great Britain, 1881 Queen Victoria £1	£30 000 unused

The top ten prices realised

Prices paid at Stanley Gibbons public auctions in London during the 1970s.

1	British Guiana 'Miss Rose' cover	£70 000
2	1851 12d on laid paper	£51 000
3	Bermuda 1848–56 'Penny Perot' on cover	£50 000
4	Mauritius 1841 penny 'Post Office'	£50 000
5	Cape of Good Hope 1861 'Woodblock' fourpenny, error of colour	£45 000
6	1851 New Carlisle 'Gaspe' colour	£31 000
7	Bermuda 1848–56 'Penny Perot'	£30 000
8	Saxony 1850 3pf, block of six	£28 000
9	British Guiana 1850–51 4c., 8c. on cover	£25 000
10	New Brunswick 1851 1/- bisect cover	£21 000

Pocket money

Beaver survey

Amount of pocket money per week; just in case you were thinking of buying some of those stamps. In order, these were the most frequent sums mentioned in our survey.

£1.00
　50p
£1.50
£2.00
　20p
　10p and 30p
　60p and £1.10
　70p
　75p
£2.50 and 40p

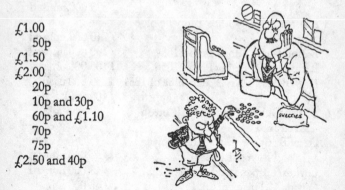

Six children out of the 600 asked said they were never given pocket money. Everybody go aahhh . . . .

Pocket money experts

According to a Gallup poll conducted for Wall's Ice-Cream, the average pocket money for 1980 across all age groups is 99p. So the children we asked must have been pretty average! The average amounts for the different age groups is as follows:

    5–7 years – 59p
    8–10 years – 66p
    11–13 years – 109p
    14–16 years – 151p

Toys

And if you have any money left, how about some toys? Or have you any old ones you want to sell? The world's most expensive set of toy soldiers, a 25-piece group of Salvation Army figures, including a band, which sold for 5/- in the Thirties, was sold at auction for £1450! However, to return to more ordinary toys. . . .

Best-selling toys of 1980

The National Association of Toy Retailers gave us this list of best-sellers – all of them nominated for the Toy of the Year Award. They are not listed in order of sales figures – just alphabetically.

Action Man
Computer Battleship
Connect
Fisher-Price Tool Kit
Legoland Space
Morris Vulcan Skates
Rubik's Cube
Cindy Electric Cooker
Space Invader
Star Wars figures

We also asked the world's largest toyshop, Hamley's of London, for their best-sellers. These toys are listed according to the volume of sales in 1980.

1 Space Invaders (electronic game)
2 Star Wars vehicles: the Millenium Falcon and the Snowspeeder
3 The Lego Space Set, especially the 928
4 Scrabble
5 Hamley's joke stockings
6 Action Man
7 The Maynard Steam Driven Train Set
8 Disco skates
9 Cindy Electric Cooker
10 Allegro (a game for classical music fans)

Top youth clubs and organisations

The Girl Guide and Boy Scout Associations continue to have the largest memberships, but the membership of youth clubs has also grown steadily.

		thousands
1	Girl Guides	360
	Boy Scouts	235
2	National Association of Youth Clubs:	
	boys	341
	girls	251
3	Boys' Brigade	147
	Girls' Brigade	103
4	YMCA	34
	YWCA	17
5	Army Cadet Corps	44
6	Combined Cadet Force	44
7	Air Training Corps	35
8	Crusaders: boys	} 22
	girls	
9	Sea Cadet Corps	19

What children would most like to be when they grow up

Beaver survey

1 policeman/woman
2 nurse
3 professional football player
4 teacher
5 doctor
6 pilot (RAF or not)
7 lorry driver
8 actor/actress
9 engineer, vet, hairdresser
10 air hostess

Only one child wanted to be an engine driver. Among the more unusual jobs were a stunt man, a political journalist, an underwater ranger in Canada, and 'anything to do with rabbits'. Hmmm.

A survey carried out by Carrick James Market Research for Wall's Ice-Cream Limited showed that among younger children, 25 per cent wanted to be professional football players, and nearly 20 per cent of girls wanted to be nurses. By school-leaving age, however, 33 per cent of boys wanted to be engineers, and the number of aspiring football stars had shrunk to 10 per cent. The ambition to join the army ranks as high as wanting to be a pop star. Nearly a quarter of the girls interviewed in their mid-teens wanted to be secretaries, and other popular careers were nursing, teaching and being an air hostess. Only 6 per cent of the girls, and even fewer of the boys, wanted to be actors or actresses.

4 Animals

Take these animal lists slowly. I'll be asking questions afterwards. What, you already knew which were the largest, the smallest, the most dangerous, the most popular, the most endangered animals in the world? I don't believe it. Well, then, I bet you haven't got the spellings right. A pity animals can't read. They could learn a lot from these lists.

The largest creatures in the world

1 Mammal – blue whale (33·58m/110ft 2½in long)
2 Bird – North African ostrich (2·74m/9ft high)
3 Reptile – estuarine or salt-water crocodile (8·23m/27ft long)
4 Amphibian – Chinese giant salamander (1·52m/5ft long)
5 Fish – Whale shark (18·5m/60ft 9in long)
6 Starfish – brisingid *Midgardia xandaros* (1380mm/54·33in tip to tip)
7 Arachnid – bird-eating spider *Theraphosa blondi* (25cm/10in leg span)

8 Crustacean – giant spider crab or stilt crab (5·79m/19ft tip to tip)
9 Insect – tropical stick-insect *Pharnacia serratipes* (330mm/13in long)
10 Centipede – *Scolopendra morsitans* (330mm/13in long)

The smallest creatures in the world

1 Mammal – Kitti's hog-nosed bat or bumblebee bat (160mm/6·29in wingspan)
2 Bird – Helena's hummingbird (58mm/2·28in long)
3 Reptile – gecko *Sphaerodactylus parthenopion* (18mm/0·71in long)
4 Amphibian – arrow-poison frog (8·5mm/0·44in long)
5 Fish – dwarf pygmy goby (7·5mm/0·28in long)
6 Starfish – *Marginaster capreenis* (20mm/0·78in diameter)
7 Arachnid – *Patu marplesi* (0·43mm/0·016in leg span)
8 Crustacean – *Alonella* (0·25mm/0·0098in tip to tip)
9 Insect – battledore-wing fairy fly (parasitic wasp) (0·2mm/0·008in long)
10 Centipede – *Lithobius dubosequi* (9·5mm/0·374in long)

The most poisonous creatures in the world

1 Snake – sea snake *Hydrophis belcheri*
2 Amphibian – arrow-poison frog
3 Fish – stonefish
4 Arachnid – black widow spider

The ten fastest animals in the world

1 Racing pigeon – 177·14 km/h (110·07 mph)
2 Spine-tailed swift – 170·99 km/h (106·25 mph)
3 Spurwing goose – 142 km/h (88 mph)
4 Peregrine falcon (132 km/h (82 mph)
5 Red-breasted merganser – 129 km/h (80 mph)
6 Sailfish – 109 km/h (68 mph)
7 Mallard – 105 km/h (65 mph)

8 Cheetah – 101+ km/h (63+ mph)
9 Pronghorn antelope – 98 km/h (61 mph)
10 Quail – 92 km/h (57 mph)

Fifteen prehistoric things alive today

1 Coelacanth (fish)
2 Australian lung fish (fish)
3 Lingula (marine animal)
4 Ginkgo (tree)
5 Peripatus (worm)
6 Horseshoe crab (crustacean)
7 Dawn redwood tree (tree)
8 Tuatara (reptile)
9 Okapi (African mammal)
10 Welwischia (desert plant)
11 Bristlecone pine (tree)
12 Stephens Island frog (amphibian)
13 Crocodile (reptile)
14 Duckbilled platypus (aquatic mammal)
15 Turtle (reptile)

The ten longest-living creatures

1 Lake sturgeon – 152 years
2 Tortoise – 116 years
3 Human being – 113 years 7 months
4 Turtle – 88 years
5 Whale – 87 years
6 Condor – 72 years
7 Elephant – 70 years
8 Raven – 69 years
9 Freshwater mussel – 60 years
10 Alligator – 56 years (and still alive in 1977)

Zoos

The most popular animals at London Zoo

In 1980, 1 500 000 people visited London Zoo – 33% were children, 40% were from overseas – and these are the animals which most people went to see.

	% of visitors
Monkeys and apes	80
Giant pandas	75
Lions	60
Tigers	60
Giraffes	45
Bears	40
Insects	30
Reptiles	30

The days of individual animals who became superstars in their own right seem to be over for the moment. In the 1950s Brumas the polar bear, London Zoo's all time great, brought in one million visitors a year. Next came Chi Chi, the giant panda in the Sixties, and then the late and greatly mourned Guy the gorilla in the Seventies.

There are two named giant pandas at present, Ching Ching and Chia Chia, but neither has caught on with the public. Zoo officials hope desperately that a baby panda will appear in the Eighties and bring in the crowds.

Total annual figures at London Zoo dropped in the Seventies, from two million in 1971 to 1·5 million in 1980. There are now 150 zoos, safari parks and bird gardens open to the public in the UK, attracting 15 million visitors a year.

Dogs

Most popular dogs' names

There are an estimated 6 million dogs in Britain: 500 000 of them in London. The National Canine Defence League have compiled the following information from the most popular selling dog identity discs which they supply to their members. The ten most popular dogs' names are:

1 Shep	6 Rover
2 Brandy	7 Skipper
3 Whisky	8 Prince
4 Patch	9 Rex
5 Butch	10 Lassie

The top five names that bitches are christened with are:

1 Sheba	4 Mandy
2 Sally	5 Tessa
3 Rosie	

Modern names: although not as popular as the old favourites like Shep and Rex, there is a growing trend towards fancier names such as Benji and Binnie. There's also a fad for Samson, Nelson and Mishka. The latter is Russian for bear and is very popular among the bigger breeds.

Twenty endangered species

1 Nubian wild ass (north-east Sudan)
2 Somali wild ass (Ethiopia)
3 Mexican grizzly bear (crest of Sierra Madre Mountains, Mexico)
4 Brander's swamp deer (Kanha National Park, Madhya Pradesh, India)
5 McNeill's deer (Tibetan plateau)
6 San Joaquin fox (San Joaquin Valley, California)
7 Northern Simien fox (Simien Mountains, Ethiopia)

8 Golden lion marmoset (south-east Brazil)
9 Northern kit fox (Cypress Hills, south-west Saskatchewan)
10 Woolly spider monkey (south-east Brazil)
11 Giant otter (eastern rivers of Brazil, Venezuela, Peru and
      Colombia)
12 Novaya Zemlya reindeer (Novaya Zemlya Island, USSR)
13 Javan rhinoceros (Java and Sumatra)
14 Northern square-lipped rhinoceros (south-west Sudan,
      Uganda, north-east Congo, western Nile Province)
15 Sumatran rhinoceros (Burma, Thailand, Malaya, Sumatra,
      Sabah and possibly India)
16 Japanese sea lion (Takeshima Island)
17 Caribbean monk seal (Caribbean area)
18 Mediterranean monk seal (Mediterranean area)
19 Blue whale (Antarctic)
20 Red wolf (Gulf coast of Texas)

5 Humour

You deserve a break, after all that learning, so what about some jokes, some stories and some lists of jokers who tell stories....

Favourite jokes

Beaver survey

We also asked children to tell us their favourite jokes. These are the most popular categories, and below are some of the better jokes from the different categories. (You should have seen the worst.)

1 knock knock
2 Irish
3 silly
4 puns
5 rude
6 sick

7 elephant
8 doctor, doctor
9 racialist, excluding Irish
10 'height of agony' (usually vulgar)

Knock knock.
'Who's there?'
'Howard.'
'Howard who?'
'Howard you like to open the door and let me in!'

Knock knock.
'Who's there?'
'Aladdin.'
'Aladdin who?'
'Aladdin the street's waiting for you!'

Did you hear about the Irish tadpole? He turned into a butter-fly.

'Doctor, doctor, I feel like a pack of cards.'
'I'll deal with you later.'

How do you make a sausage roll? Push it down a hill.

Did you hear about the Irishman in the banana factory? He threw all the bent ones away!

What did the policeman say to his chest? I've got you under a vest.

Do you have to train to be a litter collector? No, you just pick it up as you go along.

Why is the sea wet? Because the seaweed.

What did the wall say to another wall? Meet you at the corner.

Irate teacher: 'Will you pay a little attention!'
Pupil: 'I'm paying as little as possible.'

What's white and goes up in winter? An Irish snowflake.

How did the baker get an electric shock? He stood on a bun and a currant ran up his leg.

'Shall I tell you the joke about the butter?'
'No, I might spread it.'

Did you hear about the Irishman who thought rock and roll was a stone sandwich?

Two biscuits were walking down the street. One crossed the road and was run over by a car. 'Oh crumbs!' said his friend.

An Australian went into a bar and drank twelve pints of beer. At closing time when the attendant tried to throw him out he said he'd swallowed a boomerang. The attendant didn't believe him until he'd thrown him out ten times.

Did you hear about the Irishman who won the Tour de France? He did a lap of honour.

'Doctor, doctor, I feel like a pair of curtains.'
'Shut up man and pull yourself together.'

An Englishman, an Irishman and a Scotsman were asked to name one thing they would like to have with them if they were cast away on a desert island. The Englishman said 'An umbrella'; the Scotsman said 'A gun'; and the Irishman said 'A car'. When asked the reasons for their choice, the Englishman said that if it was too hot, he'd put up the umbrella and sit in its shade; the Scotsman said if it was too hot he'd shoot himself with the gun; and the Irishman said if it was too hot he'd roll down the window.

Catch phrases

Comedian Norman Vaughan made famous the catch words 'swinging' and 'dodgy' – ordinary words used in a slightly unusual way which caught the public imagination. Here are his own favourite catch phrases, listed in chronological order. (Some of them are *very* old – ask your Mum and Dad.)

1 'Can you hear me, mother?' Sandy Powell
2 'I thang yew' Arthur Askey
3 'You've deaded me, you dirty rotten swine!' Peter Sellers as Bluebottle in *The Goon Show*
4 'I've arrived, and to prove it I'm here' Max Bygraves in his radio days
5 'I'm in charge' Bruce Forsyth in *Sunday Night at the London Palladium*
6 'What do you think of it so far?'
  'Rubbish!' Morecambe and Wise
7 'Just like that!' Tommy Cooper
8 'It's goodnight from me ...'
  '... and it's goodnight from him.' The Two Ronnies
9 'Brill' and 'soopersonic' Little and Large
10 'How tickled I ham' Ken Dodd

Double acts

In the considered opinion of Little and Large, two gentlemen who appear together, this is their competition.

Little and Large's top ten double acts

1 Morecambe and Wise
2 The Two Ronnies
3 Cannon and Ball
4 Rod Hull and Emu
5 Steptoe and Son
6 George and Mildred
7 Windsor Davies and Don Estelle

8 Ronnie Dukes and Ricki Lee
9 Sooty and Sweep
10 Hinge and Bracket

Fix Its

Jimmy Savile's ten most enjoyable *Jim'll Fix It* programmes

Mr Savile receives approximately 30 000 *Fix It* letters a week. He says, 'For me it has become a way of life rather than a job and our team of workers is constantly fixing up something even if it doesn't appear on the show. Every *Jim'll Fix It*, big or small, is like a magic carpet, and very special to the kids involved.' Here are Jimmy's favourites:

1 A girl who wished to be filmed riding a white horse across the 'office atmosphere' of a news studio while a boy who wanted to be a newscaster read the news with Richard Baker: 'The only snag was the newsroom was on the sixth floor and we had to figure a way of getting the horse up there. We also had to lay some covering down in case the horse messed up the BBC floor.'
2 Mrs Howlett, a blind lady who sent in a piece of music she had herself composed which was subsequently arranged by Bob Sharples and conducted by Edward Heath.
3 Girl on a wing: an eighteen-year-old clerk wanted to stand on a wing of an aeroplane. She was assisted and trained by the Barnstormers Flying Circus: 'We had a radio mike attached to her and while she was in action we heard her say, "British Airways has nothing on this"....'
4 Wrestling with Big Daddy: a seven-year-old boy's ambition was to tag wrestle with the famous wrestler because 'Big Daddy never loses'.
5 Two girls who wanted to 'follow that cab' as in the movies were taken in a cab to Ardes in France in hot pursuit of another cab, which, when tracked down, was found to be carrying the mayor of Ardes. 'The funny thing was they'd missed the hovercraft to France so boarded the next one shouting, "follow that hovercraft"....'

6 A boy who wanted to be a butler was taken to Ragley Hall in Warwickshire, which belongs to Lord Hertford, and trained with his butler, Mr Fobbester, whom he later assisted during a dinner party given by Lord Hertford.

7 Show jumping: a little girl who transformed her parents' back garden into a mini-Hickstead with buckets, brooms and mops to construct a show-jumping course for pretend show jumping. Britain's top show jumpers Harvey Smith, David Broome and Caroline Bradley took part in the show. 'It was marvellous to see Harvey and the others jumping the course without a horse.' Raymond Brooks-Ward did the commentary.

8 A child wrote in requesting, 'Can I please polish a python,' so with the aid of some 'python polish', concocted by the *Fix It* team, a cloth and a duster, the child polished a python in the studios.

9 A girl who wanted a signed picture of Jimmy Savile was told she could take her own picture. She was taken to the RAF station in St Mawgan and flown in an RAF Nimrod over the Channel to take pictures of Jimmy Savile who was travelling on a ferry from Jersey. Jimmy signed her pictures in the studio.

10 Upstairs downstairs: octogenarian Mrs Goodenough wanted to revisit Rhinefield House where she had worked as a chambermaid in her youth. As a surprise her friends and family were invited along to dinner at the house: 'It was just like *This Is Your Life*.' She said afterwards that if she died tomorrow it was the happiest day of her life. Sadly, she died three days later.

Jokers

Jasper Carrot's funniest people

1 John Cleese
2 Blaster Bates
3 Eric Idle
4 Spike Milligan

5 Jake Thackray
6 Jeremy Taylor
7 Billy Connolly
8 Mike Harding
9 The cast of *Crossroads*

These are Mr Carrott's personal favourites in Britain. In his all-star list to joke with the Mars first eleven he would also consider the Americans Bob Newhart, Tom Lehrer, Bill Cosby, Steve Martin and George Carlin.

And now for something which could have been very similar, though only Spike Milligan is in each list. Mr Palin deliberately excluded any of his Monty Python colleagues, otherwise Mr Cleese would doubtless have featured.

Michael Palin's funniest people

1 Peter Cook
2 John Bird
3 George Segal
4 Eric Morecambe
5 Peter Nichols
6 Vladimir Nabokov
7 Evelyn Waugh
8 Spike Milligan
9 Peter Sellers
10 Geoffrey Boycott

Mr Palin's comments: 'Peter Cook undoubtedly. I like George Segal because I like actors who underplay, who don't set out deliberately to make you laugh, whose work you can quietly enjoy. Eric Morecambe has a gift for being verbally very funny, though I can see it might be hard to live with. I like Peter Nichols's plays, especially *The National Health*. Nabokov is so arrogant, but he's very funny. Every sentence is worth reading four times. I like Waugh's confidence. Spike Milligan is in as a Goon, but Sellers is there as an actor. Boycott is not meant as a joke. I genuinely think he is very funny. He produces such a wonderful reaction in other people. He upsets them utterly by being unrelenting and unhelpful. He's very Yorkshire in his public pronouncements. I think he means it all and that he's a man of humour. I'd love to see "The G. Boycott House" on TV.'

Eric Morecambe's funniest people

1 Tommy Cooper – brilliantly funny
2 Ernie Wise – rich and funny
3 Harry Worth – very funny
4 Little and Large – will be very funny
5 Kenny Everett – could be very funny
6 Cannon and Ball – they are very funny
7 Ronnie Barker – is already very funny
8 Marti Caine – oh, she's very funny
9 Two Ronnies – almost funny
10 Everybody else except Bernard Manning.

6 Biggests

You might not have found all those jokes funny, or agree about those comedians, but here are a few factual lists you can't argue about. They're not necessarily the best, but they're definitely the biggest. That's unless they happen to be the smallest . . . .

The ten tallest structures and buildings in the world

1 Warszawa Radio Mast, Poland – 646·38m (2120ft 8in)
2 C. N. Tower, Toronto – 553·3m (1822ft 1in)
3 Sears Tower, Chicago – 443m (1454ft)
4 World Trade Center, New York City – 411·48m (1350ft)
5 Empire State Building, New York City – 449m (1427ft)
6 IBA mast, Belmont, Yorkshire – 387·1m (1272ft)
7 International Nickel Company smoke stack, Sudbury, Ontario – 379·6m (1245ft 8in)
8 Drax Power Station smoke stack – 259m (850ft)

9 Lake Point Towers, Chicago – 197m (645ft)
  10 National Westminster Bank, City of London – 183m
       (600ft 4in)

The ten biggest oil tankers in the world

   1 *Pierre Guillaumat* (French flag) 414 × 62m (1359 × 206ft)
   2 *Bellamya* (French flag) 414 × 62m (1359 × 206ft)
   3 *Batillus* (French flag) 413 × 62m (1358 × 206ft)
   4 *Esso Atlantic* (Liberian flag) 406 × 71m (1333 × 233ft)
   5 *Esso Pacific* (Liberian flag) 406 × 71m (1333 × 233ft)
   6 *Nanny* (Swedish flag) 363 × 78m (1194 × 259ft)
   7 *Nissei Maru* (Japanese flag) 378 × 61m (1243 × 203ft)
   8 *Globtik London* (Liberian flag) 378 × 61m (1243 × 203ft)
   9 *Globtik Tokyo* (Liberian flag) 378 × 61m (1243 × 203ft)
  10 *Burmah Enterprise* (UK flag) 378 × 68m (1241 × 224ft)

The nine longest railway tunnels in the world

   1 Simplon, Switzerland–Italy – 19km 824m (12 miles 560 yds)
   2 Apennine, Italy – 18km 508m (11 miles 880 yds)
   3 St Gotthard, Switzerland – 14km 987m (9 miles 550 yds)
   4 Lotschberg, Switzerland – 14km 603m (9 miles 130 yds)
   5 Mont Cenis, Italy – 13km 671m (8 miles 870 yds)
   6 Cascade, USA – 12km 554m (7 miles 1410 yds)
   7 Arlberg, Austria – 10km 250m (6 miles 650 yds)
   8 Moffat, USA – 9km 839m (6 miles 220 yds)
   9 Shimizu, Japan – 9km 720m (6 miles 70 yds)

The ten longest railway tunnels in the UK

   1 Severn, Western Region – 7km 14m (4 miles 628yds)
   2 Totley, London Midland Region – 5km 697m (3 miles
       950yds)
   3 Standedge, Eastern Region – 4km 888m (3 miles 66yds)
   4 Woodhead, London Midland Region – 4km 888m (3 miles
       66yds)
   5 Sodsbury, Western Region – 4km 64m (2 miles 924 yds)

6 Disley, London Midland Region – 3km 535m (2 miles 346yds)
7 Bramhope, Eastern Region – 3km 439m (2 miles 241yds)
8 Ffestiniog, London Midland Region – 3km 528m (2 miles 338yds)
9 Cowburn, London Midland Region – 3km 386m (2 miles 182yds)
10 Sevenoaks, Southern Region – 2km 157m (1 mile 1693yds)

The ten longest bridges in the world

1 Humber Bridge, England – 2220m (7283ft)
2 Verrazano Narrows Bridge, New York – 1298m (4260ft)
3 Golden Gate Bridge, San Francisco – 1280m (4200ft)
4 Mackinac Straits Bridge, Michigan – 1158m (3800ft)
5 Bosporus, Turkey – 1074m (3523ft)
6 George Washington Bridge, New York – 1067m (3500ft)
7 Ponte Salazar (Tagus Bridge), Portugal – 1013m (3323ft)
8 Forth Road Bridge, Scotland – 1006m (3300ft)
9 Severn Bridge, England – 988m (3240ft)
10 Tacoma Bridge, Washington, USA – 853m (2800ft)

The nine longest rivers in the world

1 Nile – 6670km (4145 miles)
2 Amazon – 6448km (4007 miles)
3 Mississippi – 5970km (3710 miles)
4 Yenisey-Algara-Selenga – 5540km (3442 miles)
5 Yangtze Kiang – 5530km (3436 miles)
6 Ob'-Irtysh – 5410 km (3362 miles)
7 Hwang Ho (Yellow River) – 4830km (3000 miles)
8 Zaire (Congo) – 4700km (2920 miles)
9 Lena-Kiringa – 4400km (2734 miles)

The ten longest rivers in the UK

1 Severn – 355km (220 miles)
2 Thames – 338km (210 miles)
3 Trent – 300km (185 miles)
4 Aire – 260km (161 miles)
5 Ouse – 230km (143 miles)
6 Wye – 215km (135 miles)
7 Tay – 188km (117 miles)
8 Nene – 161km (100 miles)
9 Clyde – 158km (98·5 miles)
10 Spey – 157·5km (98 miles)

The ten highest mountains in the world

1 Mount Everest – 8848m (29 028ft)
2 K2 (Chogori) – 8610m (28 250ft)
3 Kangchenjunga – 8597m (28 208ft)
4 Lhotse – 8511m (27 923ft)
5 Yalung Kang, Kangchenjunga West – 8502m (27 894ft)
6 Yalung Kang, Kangchenjunga South Peak – 8488m (27 848ft)
7 Makalu 1 – 8481m (27 824ft)
8 Kangchenjunga Middle Peak – 8475m (27 806ft)
9 Lhotse Shar – 8383m (27 504ft)
10 Dhaulargiri 1 – 8167m (26 795ft)

The ten highest mountains in the UK

1 Ben Nevis, Highland – 1392m (4406ft)
2 Ben Macdhui, Grampian – 1310m (4300ft)
3 Braeriach, Grampian-Highland border – 1294m (4248ft)
4 Cairn Toul, Grampian – 1292m (4241ft)
5 Cairngorm, Grampian-Highland border – 1244m (4084ft)
6 Aonach Beag – 1237m (4060ft)
7 Carn Mor Dearg, Highland – 1222m (4012ft)
8 Aonach Mor, Highland – 1218m (3999ft)
9 Ben Lawers, Tayside – 1214m (3984ft)
10 Beinn à Bhùird (North Top), Grampian – 1196m (3924ft)

The ten biggest countries in the world

1 USSR – 22 402 200 sq km (8 649 489 sq miles)
2 Canada – 9 976 139 sq km (3 851 787 sq miles)
3 China (mainland) – 9 561 000 sq km (3 691 502 sq miles)
4 USA – 9 363 123 sq km (3 615 102 sq miles)
5 Brazil – 8 511 965 sq km (3 286 470 sq miles)
6 Australia – 7 682 300 sq km (2 966 136 sq miles)
7 India – 3 287 590 sq km (1 269 338 sq miles)
8 Argentina – 2 776 889 sq km (1 072 157 sq miles)
9 Sudan – 2 505 813 sq km (967 494 sq miles)
10 Algeria – 2 381 741 sq km (919 590 sq miles)

The ten smallest countries in the world

1 Vatican City – 0·44 sq km (0·17 sq miles)
2 Monaco – 1·81 sq km (0·70 sq miles)
3 Nauru – 21 sq km (8·1 sq miles)
4 Tuvala – 24·6 sq km (9·5 sq miles)
5 San Marino – 60·5 sq km (23·4 sq miles)
6 Liechtenstein – 160 sq km (61·2 sq miles)
7 Maldives – 298 sq km (115 sq miles)
8 Seychelles – 308 sq km (119 sq miles)
9 Malta – 316 sq km (122 sq miles)
10 Grenada – 344 sq km (133 sq miles)

The ten biggest lakes in the world

1 Caspian Sea – 371 800 sq km (143 550 sq miles)
2 Superior – 82 350 sq km (31 800 sq miles)
3 Victoria Nyanza – 69 500 sq km (26 828 sq miles)
4 Aral'skaya More (Aral Sea) – 65 500 sq km (25 300 sq miles)
5 Huron – 59 600 sq km (23 010 sq miles)
6 Michigan – 58 000 sq km (22 400 sq miles)
7 Tanganyika – 32 900 sq km (12 700 sq miles)
8 Great Bear – 31 800 sq km (12 275 sq miles)
9 Ozero Baykal – 30 500 sq km (11 780 sq miles)
10 Malawi – 29 600 sq km (11 430 sq miles)

The ten biggest lakes in the UK

1 Lough Neagh, Northern Ireland – 381·7 sq km (147·4 sq miles)
2 Lower Lough Erne, Northern Ireland – 105 sq km (40·6 sq miles)
3 Loch Lomond, Scotland – 71·2 sq km (27·5 sq miles)
4 Loch Ness, Scotland – 56·6 sq km (21·9 sq miles)
5 Loch Awe, Scotland – 38·7 sq km (14·9 sq miles)
6 Upper Lough Erne, Northern Ireland – 31·7 sq km (12·25 sq miles)
7 Loch Mareg, Scotland – 28·4 sq km (11 sq miles)
8 Loch Morar, Scotland – 26·6 sq km (10·3 sq miles)
9 Loch Tay, Scotland – 26·3 sq km (10·19 sq miles)
10 Loch Shin, Scotland – 22·5 sq km (8·7 sq miles)

World weather

The **hottest** place in the world is Dallol, Ethiopia, where the annual mean temperature is 34·4°C (94°F). The highest world shade temperature recorded was at Al' Aziziyah, Libya, in 1922: 58°C (136·4°F).

The **coldest** place in the world is Polus Nedostupnosti, or the Pole of Cold, Antarctica, where the annual mean temperature is −57·8°C (−72°F). The coldest temperature recorded was at Vostok, Antarctica, in 1960: −88·3°C (−126·9°F).

The **wettest** place in the world is Mt Wai-'ale-'ale, Hawaii, where the annual rainfall is 11 455mm (451in) (average for 1970–72).

The **driest** place in the world is the Desierto de Atacama in Chile, where the annual mean rainfall is nil.

The **windiest** place in the world is The Commonwealth Bay on George V Coast, Antarctica, where gales reach 320 km/h (200 mph).

The **foggiest** place in the world is Grand Banks, Newfoundland, Canada, which has, on average, more than 120 days of fog per year.

The **sunniest** place in the world is the eastern Sahara Desert, which averages over 4300 hours of sunshine per year.

The **snowiest** place in the world is Mt Rainier, Washington, USA, where 31 102mm (1224·5in) of snow fell between February 1971 and February 1972.

The ten most populated countries in the world

1 China (mainland) – 958 094 000
2 India – 638 388 000
3 USSR – 262 442 000
4 USA – 218 502 000
5 Indonesia – 130 597 000
6 Brazil – 115 397 000
7 Japan – 114 898 000
8 Bangladesh – 84 655 000
9 Pakistan – 76 770 000
10 Nigeria – 72 220 000

The ten least populated countries in the world

1 Vatican City – 1000
2 Nauru – 7254
3 Tuvalu – 9000
4 San Marino – 20 400
5 Liechtenstein – 24 715
6 Monaco – 25 029
7 Andorra – 29 000
8 Kiribati – 51 929
9 Seychelles – 61 898
10 Dominica – 80 000

The ten most populated cities in the world

1 Tokyo, Japan (1977) – 11 688 313
2 Shanghai, China (1976) – 10 000 000
3 Mexico City, Mexico (1976) – 8 941 912
4 Buenos Aires, Argentina (1970) – 8 774 529
5 Cairo, Egypt (1975) – 8 143 000
6 Moscow, USSR (1979) – 8 011 000
7 Peking, China (1976) – 8 000 000
8 New York, USA (1970) – 7 895 563
9 Seoul, Korea (1978) – 7 823 195
10 Tientsin, China (1976) – 7 000 000

The ten most populated cities in the UK

(1978 census)

1 London – 6 918 000
2 Birmingham – 1 060 800
3 Glasgow – 830 000
4 Leeds – 733 800
5 Sheffield – 555 400
6 Liverpool – 542 100
7 Manchester – 491 700
8 Edinburgh – 467 097
9 Bradford – 458 300
10 Bristol – 416 300

Biggest English counties

This also gives you an extra list for the price of one – a list of
all the English counties with their correct names.

	acres
Yorkshire, North	2 053 126
Cumbria	1 682 239
Devonshire	1 658 285
Lincolnshire	1 454 351
Norfolk	1 323 371

Northumberland	1 243 692
Hereford and Worcestershire	970 203
Suffolk	940 800
Hampshire	934 474
Kent	922 196
Essex	907 850
Cornwall	876 295
Humberside	867 784
Shropshire	862 479
Wiltshire	860 109
Somerset	852 434
Cambridgeshire	842 433
Lancashire	751 063
Staffordshire	671 184
Dorset	655 818
Gloucestershire	652 741
Derbyshire	650 146
Oxfordshire	645 314
Leicestershire	630 842
Durham	601 939
Northamptonshire	584 970
Cheshire	575 375
Nottinghamshire	534 735
Yorkshire, West	503 863
Sussex, West	498 178
Warwickshire	489 405
Buckinghamshire	465 019
Sussex, East	443 634
Surrey	414 922
Hertfordshire	403 787
Greater London	390 302
Yorkshire, South	385 605
Avon	332 596
Greater Manchester	317 285
Berkshire	310 178
Bedfordshire	305 026
West Midlands	222 258
Merseyside	159 750
Cleveland	144 086

Tyne and Wear	133 390
Isle of Wight	94 134

Most populated English counties

Greater London	6 918 100
West Midlands	2 711 600
Greater Manchester	2 663 500
Yorkshire, West	2 067 900
Merseyside	1 545 500
Hampshire	1 453 400
Kent	1 449 000
Essex	1 435 600
Lancashire	1 369 600
Yorkshire, South	1 304 100
Tyne and Wear	1 165 100
Staffordshire	997 000
Surrey	995 400
Nottinghamshire	973 700
Devonshire	948 000
Hertfordshire	947 100
Avon	921 900
Cheshire	919 800
Derbyshire	896 200
Humberside	844 900
Leicestershire	833 300
Norfolk	679 800
Berkshire	672 600
Yorkshire, North	661 300
Sussex, East	652 500
Sussex, West	633 600
Hereford and Worcestershire	610 100
Durham	603 800
Suffolk	592 700
Dorset	586 500
Cambridgeshire	570 200
Cleveland	568 200
Oxfordshire	540 600
Lincolnshire	530 100

Buckinghamshire	525 100
Northamptonshire	516 400
Wiltshire	516 200
Gloucestershire	495 300
Bedfordshire	494 700
Cumbria	472 400
Warwickshire	469 500
Cornwall	416 700
Somerset	411 100
Shropshire	365 900
Northumberland	289 200
Isle of Wight	114 300

Top ten English counties in order of population density

		people per acre
1	Greater London	17·72
2	West Midlands	12·20
3	Merseyside	9·67
4	Tyne and Wear	8·73
5	Greater Manchester	8·39
6	Yorkshire, West	4·10
7	Cleveland	3·94
8	Yorkshire, South	3·38
9	Avon	2·77
10	Hertfordshire	2·35

Bottom ten English counties in order of population density

		people per acre
1	Northumberland	0·23
2	Cumbria	0·28
3	Yorkshire, North	0·32
4	Lincolnshire	0·36
5	Shropshire	0·42
6	Cornwall	0·48

7	Somerset	0·48	
8	Norfolk	0·51	
9	Devonshire	0·57	
10	Wiltshire	0·60	

Just to finish off the population lists, here's the UK population. You can have a rest soon.

UK population

	millions		*projections*
1901	38·2	1981	55·9
1911	42·1	1986	56·3
1921	44·0	1991	57·0
1931	46·0	1996	57·7
1941	48·2	2001	58·0
1951	50·5		
1961	53·0		
1971	55·7		
1978	55·9		

Heaviest MPs

The General Election in May 1979 brought in a good new batch of fatties, to join the existing heavyweights, but no one quite reached Cyril Smith's proportions and he remains the outright winner in this brand-new contest. The weights are all estimates, but based on first-hand observation by a well-known parliamentary expert, who wishes to remain anonymous, just in case anyone sits on him. (Any MP who feels he has been misused should furnish proof of his correct weight.)

Cyril Smith	27	stones
Iain Mills	20	,,
Donald Thompson	18	,,
Peter Emery	18	,,
Rev. Ian Paisley	18	,,
Martin Stevens	18	,,
Geraint Morgan	17	,,

Eric Heffer	17	,,
Russell Kerr	17	,,
Harry Cowans	17	,,
Edward Heath	17	,,
Geoffrey Dickens	16	,,
Graham Bright	16	,,
Hector Monroe	16	,,
Michael Jopling	16	,,
Robert Taylor	16	,,
Spencer le Marchant	16	,,
John Stokes	16	,,

The ten heaviest people in the world

1 Robert Earl Hughes (USA, 1926–58) – 485kg (76st 5lb)
2 Mills Darden (USA, 1798–1857) – 463kg (72st 12lb)
3 John Hanson Craig (USA, 1856–94) – 411kg (64st 11lb)
4 Arthur Knorr (USA, 1914–60) – 408kg (64st 4lb)
   John Minnoch (USA, 1941–   ) – 408kg (64st 4lb)
5 Toubi (Cameroon, 1946–   ) – 389kg (61st 3½lb)
6 T. A. Valenzuela (USA, 1895–1937) – 386 kg (60st 10lb)
7 Flora Mae Jackson (USA, 1930–65) – 381kg (60st)
8 David Maguire (USA, 1904–35) – 367kg (57st 12lb)
9 William J. Cobb (USA, 1926–   ) – 363kg (57st 4lb)

7 People

An assortment of people who have done early, awful and famous things. . . .

Child prodigies

Compiled by Mr George Mell

Don't read this if you suffer from an inferiority complex.

At the age of
Three months Jean Louis Cardiac, of France, could repeat the alphabet. At three years he could read Latin and at four could translate it into French or English.
Four months Kenneth Wolf, of Cleveland, Ohio, spoke his first words. At two and a half years he played his first notes on the piano. At three he started studying chemistry.
One year Christian Heinecken, of Lubeck, Germany, could repeat long passages from the Bible. At two and a half he spoke Latin, French and German and began learning Greek.

Two years Thomas Young, of Milverton, Somerset, could read.

Three years John Stuart Mill, English economist and philosopher, read Greek. At five years he learned Latin and at eight years studied higher mathematics.

Four years Thomas Babington Macaulay wrote a history of the world and at eight years composed a treatise on how to convert the natives of Malabar to Christianity.

Five years Joseph Burke, of Ireland, was a popular actor in Dublin, playing adult roles, including Hamlet.

Six years Mozart composed short pieces for the harpsichord and completed a piano concerto.

Seven years Truman Stafford, of England, studied algebra and geometry and, soon after, higher mathematics and astronomy.

Eight years Paganini, violinist, composed a sonata so difficult that few except himself could play it.

Nine years William James Sidis, of the USA, spoke French, English, German, Latin and Greek, and at eleven years addressed a meeting of professors on the fourth dimension.

Ten years George Parker Bidder, of England, was a famous lightning calculator. In a test he was asked what was the compound interest on £4444 for 4444 days at $4\frac{1}{2}\%$ per annum and gave the correct answer – £2434 16s $5\frac{1}{4}$d.

Eleven years Mendelssohn had written over fifty compositions, including an operetta, sonata for piano and violin, a cantata, chamber music and pieces for the organ.

Makes you sick, doesn't it. . . .

Kings and queens

Longest-reigning English monarchs

1	Queen Victoria	63 years
2	George III	59 ,,
3	Henry III	56 ,,
4	Edward III	50 ,,

5	Elizabeth I	44	,,
6	Henry VI	39	,,
7	Henry VIII	38	,,
8	Ethelred II	37	,,
9	Charles II	36	,,
10	Henry I	35	,,
11	Edward I	35	,,
12	Henry II	35	,,
13	George II	33	,,

Shortest-reigning English monarchs

1	Lady Jane Grey	14 days
2	Edward V	75 ,,
3	Edward VIII	325 ,,
4	Ethelbald	2 years
5	Hardicanute	2 ,,
6	Richard III	2 ,,
7	Edwy	3 ,,
8	James II	3 ,,
9	Edward the Martyr	4 ,,
10	Ethelred I	5 ,,
11	Harold I	5 ,,
12	Mary I	5 ,,

The ten youngest monarchs to succeed to the throne in England

1 Henry III (1216–72) – aged nine
2 Henry VI (1422–61) – aged ten
3 Edward VI (1547–53) – aged ten
4 Ethelred II (978–1016) – aged eleven
5 Richard II (1377–99) – aged eleven
6 Edward the Martyr (975–8) – aged thirteen
7 Edward V (1483–83, 75 days) – aged thirteen
8 Edwy (955–9) – aged fifteen
9 Edgar (959–75) – aged fifteen
10 Edward III (1327–77) – aged fifteen

71

The ten first men in space

1 Yuri Alekseyevich Gagarin (USSR, 12 April 1961)
2 Alan B. Shepard (US, 5 May 1961)
3 Virgil Ivan Grissom (US, 21 July 1961)
4 Gherman Stepanovich Titov (USSR, 6–7 August 1961)
5 John Herschel Glenn (US, 20 February 1962)
6 Malcolm Scott Carpenter (US, 24 May 1962)
7 Andrian Grigorievich Nikolayev (USSR, 11–15 August 1962)
8 Pavel Romanovich Popovich (USSR, 12–15 August 1962)
9 Walter Marty Schirra (US, 3 October 1962)
10 Larry Gordon Cooper (US, 15–16 May 1963)

Blue plaque people

GLC figures

There are 439 blue plaques on London houses, commemorating the fact that some famous person once lived there. Some lucky people are remembered by more than one plaque, having lived in different houses.

Three plaques

Henry Fielding	novelist
W. E. Gladstone	statesman
D. G. Rossetti	poet and painter
Lord Palmerston	statesman
W. M. Thackeray	novelist

Two plaques

John Logie Baird	television pioneer
Sir J. M. Barrie	novelist and dramatist
Elizabeth Barrett Browning	poet
Sir Isambard Kingdom Brunel	civil engineer
Joseph Chamberlain	statesman
Samuel Taylor Coleridge	poet
Benjamin Disraeli	statesman
George du Maurier	artist and writer
George Eliot	novelist

John Galsworthy	novelist
David Garrick	actor
W. S. Gilbert	dramatist
John Richard Green	historian
Thomas Hardy	novelist
Thomas Hood	poet
W. R. Lethaby	architect
William Morris	poet and artist
Lord Nelson	admiral
Samuel Pepys	diarist
George Bernard Shaw	dramatist
Richard Brinsley Sheridan	dramatist
Sir Hans Sloane	physician
Algernon Swinburne	poet
William Wilberforce	philanthropist

Total number of plaques in each London borough

Westminster	179
Kensington and Chelsea	84
Camden	71
Wandsworth	18
Hammersmith	13
Tower Hamlets	11
Lambeth	10
Greenwich	8
Islington	8
Lewisham	6
Croydon	4
Richmond	4
Southwark	4
Hackney	3
Haringey	3
Harrow	3
Barnet	2
Bexley	1
Brent	1

Bromley	1
Ealing	1
Hounslow	1
Merton	1
Redbridge	1
Sutton	1

Heroes and heroines

Carrick James Market Research recently did a survey for Wall's Ice-Cream Limited, asking children 'Which person alive today do you most admire?' This is what they said:

1	Kevin Keegan	7 per cent
2	John Travolta	3 per cent
3	Cliff Richard	3 per cent
4	Kenny Dalglish	2 per cent
5	Debbie Harry	2 per cent
6	The Queen	2 per cent
7	Clint Eastwood	2 per cent
8	John Cleese	2 per cent
9	Jimmy Savile	2 per cent
10	Wonder Woman (L. Carter)	2 per cent
11	'My mum'	1 per cent
12	others*	55 per cent
	don't know	17 per cent

* No other individual had enough votes to warrant a 1 per cent share in this table.

Poets laureate

1 John Dryden, 1668–88
2 Thomas Shadwell, 1688–92
3 Nahum Tate, 1692–1715
4 Nicholas Rowe, 1715–18
5 Laurence Eusden, 1718–30
6 Colley Cibber, 1730–57
7 William Whitehead, 1757–85

8 Thomas Warton, 1785–90
9 Henry James Pye, 1790–1813
10 Robert Southey, 1813–34
11 William Wordsworth, 1843–50
12 Alfred, Lord Tennyson, 1850–92
13 Alfred Austin, 1896–1913
14 Robert Bridges, 1913–30
15 John Masefield, 1930–67
16 Cecil Day-Lewis, 1968–72
17 Sir John Betjeman, 1972–

Villains

And certainly don't read this if you scare easily.

Lesser known British villains (in no particular order)

Jonathon Green, compiler of The Directory of Infamy

1 **Kate Webster** Preferred drinking to housework. She killed her employer after being told off, then dismembered the corpse, boiled up the flesh and dumped it by the river near Hammersmith. She sold the rendered human dripping around the local pubs. Arrested in her native Ireland in 1879, she was hanged.

2 **Sawney Beane** The Beane family – some forty-six, all incestuous, flourished near Galloway, Scotland, in the late fourteenth century. At the time of their capture in 1435 they had killed and robbed some 1000 victims. The authorities caught up with them and the family were killed slowly and painfully. Their victims' corpses, butchered and smoked, festooned the Beane's cavernous HQ.

3 **The Reverend Harold Davidson**, Rector of Stiffkey. The hapless cleric was discovered consorting with London prostitutes, thus scandalising his Norfolk parish in the 1930s. He was defrocked and turned to show-business, appearing in a tub and placing his head in a lion's mouth in fairgrounds round the country. The lion duly shut its jaws one sad day in Skegness.

4 **Mary Ann Cotton** Britain's premiere mass murderer managed at least sixteen and probably twenty-one victims – all close relatives – between 1852 and 1872. All apparently suffered from 'gastric fever'. Mary was hanged in 1873, a job which was bungled and took three minutes.

5 **Richard Rosse** Rosse was cook to the Bishop of Rochester in 1531. For undisclosed reasons he poisoned some seventeen of the bishop's guests at a dinner. Rosse was boiled to death for his crime.

6 **Horace Rayner** Rayner was the unacknowledged illegitimate son of William Whiteley, 'the Universal Provider' and founder of Whiteley's department store in Queensway, W2. In 1907 he walked into his father's office, argued with him, then shot him dead. Whiteley's motto 'Add conscience to your capital' had not extended to his private life, but 20 000 people signed a petition and saved his son from the gallows. Rayner still served twelve years.

7 **Arthur Furguson** Furguson, an erstwhile actor, used his talents for special solo performances. He sold Nelson's column at £6000 a time, and 'rented out' Buckingham Palace and the Tower of London. In 1925 he moved to America. After many successes he was jailed when he failed to sell the Statue of Liberty for $100 000. Released from jail in 1930, he vanished.

8 **Mary Tofts** In 1726 this simple country girl from Godalming, Surrey, managed to persuade a large number of people who should have known better that she had given birth to rabbits. She produced a number of litters and convinced even M St André, the king's surgeon. Finally the imposture was discovered and she was packed off to the country.

8 Places

Uplifting places, in the main, which you should certainly try to visit. How many have you been to already? Don't lie, because our spies are everywhere. . . .

Galleries and museums

Attendances at major art galleries and museums

Art Galleries	1966	1971	1976	1977	1978
			thousands		
National Gallery	1521	1859	2354	2686	2501
Tate Gallery	894	936	1202	1006	1081
Royal Academy	300	250	389	1150	850
National Portrait Gallery	248	513	324	535	425
Hayward Gallery		137	414	92	342
Scottish National Gallery	207	241	175	171	235
Serpentine Gallery		55	132	173	229

| | | | *thousands* | | |
Museums	1966	1971	1976	1977	1978
British Museum	1808	2680	3964	4124	4034
Science Museum	1700	1942	2508	3361	3486
Natural History Museum	1059	1576	2703	3193	2788
Victoria and Albert Museum	1322	2034	1552	2340	1934
National Railway Museum, York			1830	1440	1486
Imperial War Museum	431	557	726	1090	1435
National Maritime Museum	786	1591	1700	1250	1260
Royal Scottish Museum	533	534	608	611	646
Geological Museum	367	345	496	510	531
National Museum of Wales	372	383	287	337	328
Welsh Folk Museum	123	185	285	269	288

We asked the following London galleries and museums which were their most popular children's exhibitions or exhibits. This is what they said:

National Gallery Three times a year the National Gallery gives out quiz sheets on a specific theme to children. The most popular have been those on monsters and creepy-crawlies; animals were the second most popular.

National Portrait Gallery Among the children's projects they have carried out, the one on the Tudors was the most popular with all ages.

Royal Academy *The Light Fantastic* (January to March 1978) was the most popular exhibition of all; the Post-Impressionism exhibition from November 1979 to March 1980 was also very popular, with 67 000 schoolchildren and student visitors.

Natural History Museum Over a quarter of a million schoolchildren visit the museum every year. Dinosaurs are the most popular exhibits with primary schoolchildren; with secondary schoolchildren 40 per cent of each party visits the human biology section and 40 per cent visits the ecology section.

Science Museum Among their Christmas lectures, which are mostly geared to children, *Twenty-one Years of the Mini* and *Microchip* have been the most popular so far.

Victoria and Albert Museum Their Christmas exhibitions are the most popular with children; favourites have been Beatrix Potter's costumes and illustrations for *The Tailor of Gloucester*, 1976; *The Makers* (craftsmen working in the museum), 1975; *Body Box*, 1974; *Pack Age* and the Wombles exhibition, 1975.

Historic sights

Historic buildings attracting more than 200 000 paid admissions in 1978

English Tourist Board

NB Historic buildings to which entry is free, such as Westminster Abbey, are not included in this list.

Tower of London	3 005 000
State apartments, Windsor Castle	940 000
Stonehenge, Wiltshire	795 000
Roman Baths and Pump Room, Bath, Avon	794 000
St George's Chapel, Windsor, Berkshire	700 000
Hampton Court, London	660 000
Beaulieu, Hampshire	649 000
Shakespeare's birthplace, Warwickshire	640 000
Warwick Castle, Warwickshire	517 000
Anne Hathaway's Cottage, Warwickshire	479 000
Royal Pavilion, Brighton, East Sussex	409 000
Salisbury Cathedral, Wiltshire	378 000
Osborne House, Isle of Wight	292 000
Harewood House, West Yorkshire	273 000
Fountains Abbey, North Yorkshire	240 000
Dodington House, Avon	228 000
Brontë Parsonage, Haworth, West Yorkshire	214 000
Dover Castle, Kent	214 000
Assembly Rooms, Bath, Avon	207 000

Blenheim Palace, Chatsworth, Longleat and Woburn Abbey – all privately owned homes – do not reveal admissions, but they each had over 200 000 visitors in 1978.

National Parks

There are now ten National Parks in England and Wales, areas of national beauty and importance which were designated as such and given certain legal safeguards under a 1949 Act. They now cover 9% of the land surface.

The idea came from the USA. Most European countries had them years before England and Wales; Scotland still has none.

National Parks in England and Wales – in acres

(date of origin in brackets)

1 Lake District (17 April 1951)	554 240
2 Snowdonia (18 October 1951)	540 800
3 Yorkshire Dales (12 October 1954)	435 200
4 North Yorkshire Moors (28 November 1952)	353 920
5 Peak District (17 April 1951)	346 880
6 Brecon Beacons (17 April 1957)	332 160
7 Northumberland (6 April 1956)	254 720
8 Dartmoor (30 October 1951)	233 600
9 Exmoor (19 October 1954)	169 600
10 Pembrokeshire (29 February 1952)	144 000

Cathedrals

The most popular

In order, these are the most visited cathedrals in England based on attendance figures. The figures, which refer to 1977 and come from the English Tourist Board, are in many cases estimates. Westminster Abbey, the No 1, is not technically a cathedral, nor are King's College Chapel, Bath Abbey, Beverley Minster, Selby Abbey, Tewkesbury Abbey nor St George's Chapel, Windsor, but the ETB calls them 'greater churches' and lumps them with the 40 official cathedrals in their 1979 book on English cathedrals.

Westminster Abbey	3 million+
St Paul's, London	2 million+
Canterbury Cathedral	1 million+
York Minster	1 million+
King's College Chapel, Cambridge	1 million
St George's Chapel, Windsor	1 million
Coventry	666 000
Salisbury	500 000
Durham	500 000
Chester	450 000
Exeter	375 000
Lincoln	375 000
Norwich	375 000
Oxford	375 000
Wells	375 000
Winchester	375 000
Ely	300 000
Westminster RC	250 000
St Albans	250 000
Bath Abbey	250 000
Worcester	200 000
Chichester	200 000
Gloucester	200 000
Truro	200 000
Carlisle	150 000
Ripon	150 000
Hereford	100 000
Bury St Edmunds	100 000
Guildford	100 000
Lichfield	100 000
Peterborough	100 000
Rochester	100 000
Beverley Minster	75 000
Tewkesbury Abbey	60 000
Bristol	60 000
Liverpool C of E	60 000
Southwell	60 000
Southwark	50 000
Arundel RC	45 000

Sheffield	40 000
Manchester	40 000
Newcastle	30 000
Selby	30 000
Liverpool RC	25 000
Portsmouth	20 000
Leicester	8 000
Bradford	4 000

9 Entertainment

Some facts and opinions about pop music, films, TV, comics and books. (This book wasn't published when we did our survey of favourite children's books or it would have been *terribly* high.)

Favourite pop star or group

This is what the people in the Beaver survey said anyway.

1 The Police
2 ABBA
3 Madness
4 Elvis Presley
5 Cliff Richard
6 Blondie
7 Kelly Marie and Boomtown Rats
8 The Jam
9 Kate Bush and Showaddywaddy
10 Bad Manners, The Sex Pistols, ELO, Status Quo and Diana Ross

Pop music

The top best-selling singles in the UK since 1960

Record Business

1 'Mull of Kintyre', Wings (1977)
2 'Rivers of Babylon', Boney M (1978)
3 'You're the One That I Want', John Travolta and Olivia Newton John (1978)
4 'Mary's Boy Child', Boney M (1978)
5 'She Loves You', The Beatles (1963)
6 'I Wanna Hold Your Hand', The Beatles (1963)
7 'Tears', Ken Dodd (1965)
8 'Summer Nights', John Travolta and Olivia Newton John (1978)
9 'Can't Buy Me Love', The Beatles (1964)
10 'I Feel Fine', The Beatles (1964)
11 'The Carnival Is Over', The Seekers (1965)
12 'We Can Work It Out'/'Day Tripper', The Beatles (1965)
13 'Bright Eyes', Art Garfunkel (1979)
14 'Y.M.C.A.', Village People (1979)
15 'Bohemian Rhapsody', Queen (1975)
16 'Please Release Me', Engelbert Humperdinck (1967)
17 'It's Now Or Never', Elvis Presley (1960)
18 'Heart of Glass', Blondie (1979)
19 'Green Green Grass of Home', Tom Jones (1966)
20 'I Love You, Love Me', Gary Glitter (1973)

The Beatles monopolize the chart with five singles, and Paul McCartney tops it with the two-million seller 'Mull of Kintyre'. But Ken Dodd managed to outsell the Beatles in 1965 when 'Tears' was released. Boney M put the only Christmas single in the Top Twenty with 'Mary's Boy Child', first made popular by Harry Belafonte – a song written by Jester Hairston who played the butler in *In the Heat of the Night*.

Single sales peaked in 1964 thanks to the Beatles and the Mersey boom, when 73 million singles were sold.

The top ten albums of the Seventies

British Market Research Bureau

1 'Bridge Over Troubled Water', Simon and Garfunkel
2 Abba's 'Greatest Hits'
3 'Tubular Bells', Mike Oldfield
4 Simon and Garfunkel's 'Greatest Hits'
5 'Saturday Night Fever', The Bee Gees
6 'The Singles 1969–73', The Carpenters
7 'Arrival', Abba
8 'Dark Side of the Moon', Pink Floyd
9 Original soundtrack from *Grease*
10 Elvis Presley's '40 Greatest Hits'

The most popular albums, 1980

Record Business

Coming more up to date, these were the best-selling pop albums in 1980. It remains to be seen how many, if any, become all-time best-sellers.

1 'Zenyatta Mondatta', Police
2 'Super Trouper', Abba
3 'Guilty', Barbra Streisand
4 'Reggatta de Blanc', Police
5 'Flesh and Blood', Roxy Music
6 'Manilow Magic', Barry Manilow
7 'Greatest Hits', Rose Royce
8 'Off the Wall', Michael Jackson
9 'Duke', Genesis
10 'Sky 2', Sky

Worst records ever

Kenny Everett, the well-known TV and radio person, asked his listeners on Capital Radio to send him their very worst records, so that he could play them, then smash them. In 1978 a total of 3210 listeners wrote in – these are the worst records in order of nominations cast.

1	'I Want my Baby Back', Jimmy Cross	510
2	'Wunderbar', Zarah Leander	506
3	'Paralysed', The Legendary Stardust Cowboy	310
4	'The Deal', Pat Campbell	295
5	'Transfusion', Nervous Norvus	117
6	'This Pullover', Jess Conrad	102
7	'Spinning Wheel', Mel and Dave	98
8	'Laurie', Dickie Lee	90
9	'A Lover's Concerto', Mrs Miller	84
10	'I Get So Lonely', Tanya Day	83
11	'The Drunken Driver', Ferlin Husky	80
12	'Runk Bunk', Adam Faith	78
13	'Why Am I Living?' Jess Conrad	72
14	'29th September', Equipe 84	70
15	'Surfin' Bird', The Trashmen	69
16	'Let's Get Together', Hayley Mills	66
17	'Mechanical Man', Bent Bolt and The Nuts	60
18	'I'm Going to Spain', Steve Bent	58
19	'The Big Architect', Duncan Johnson	57
20	'Cherry Pie', Jess Conrad	52
21	'Dottie', Mickie Most	50
22	'Kinky Boots', Patrick MacNee and Honor Blackman	49
23	'The Shifting, Whispering Sands', Eamonn Andrews	46
24	'My Girl', Floyd Robinson	40
25	'Revelation', Daniel	37
26	'Going Out of my Head', Raphael	32
27	'Made You', Don Duke	30

28 'My Feet Start Tapping', Adolf Babel   27
29 'Hey Little Girl', Ray Sharpe   23
30 'The Puppet Song', Hughie Green   20

Just to show you what a nice person cuddly Ken really is, here are his own favourite tunes.

Kenny Everett's favourites

1 Tchaikovsky's March from Pathétique Symphony
2 Brahms's Violin Concerto in D, opus 77
3 Bizet's Symphony in C, 4th Movement
4 'Steppin' Out' (from 'Out of the Blue' by ELO)
5 'Big Wheels' (from 'Out of the Blue' by ELO)
6 'Sweet is the Night' (from 'Out of the Blue' by ELO)
7 'I'd Rather Leave While I'm in Love', Carole Bayer Sager
8 'Blue Suede Shoes', Elvis Presley
9 Mendelssohn's Violin Concerto in E minor
10 'Strawberry Fields Forever', The Beatles

Favourite films

Beaver survey

1 *Star Wars*
2 *The Empire Strikes Back*
3 James Bond films, especially *Moonraker* and *The Spy Who Loved Me*
4 *Grease*
5 *Jaws* and *Jaws II*
6 *The Love Bug, Buck Rogers in the 25th Century* and *Close Encounters of the Third Kind*
7 *The Sound of Music, Airplane* and *Watership Down*
8 *Smokey and the Bandit, Superman* and Elvis Presley films
9 *Battlestar Galactica, Tarka the Otter* and *The Black Hole*
10 *The Magnificent Seven*

ABC Cinemas report that the most popular films at Saturday matinees are *Superman, Watership Down, Warlords of Atlantis* and *Battlestar Galactica*.

Radio requests

We asked Don George, Producer of *Junior Choice*, which receives the biggest postbag in BBC Radio – 2400 letters a week – which were the records most requested. Obviously the choice reflects the charts, and he said that ABBA were the most popular artists ever, though records by the Smurfs, the Wombles and the Muppets were much requested. In the mid-Seventies the Osmonds and David Cassidy were most popular. But the list of all-time favourites, arranged in order of the age of the record, is as follows:

1 'The Laughing Policeman' by Charles Penrose
2 'Nellie the Elephant' by Mandy Miller
3 'Rupert the Bear' by Jackie Lee
4 'My Brother' by Terry Scott
5 'The Runaway Train' by Michael Holliday
6 'Two Little Boys' by Rolf Harris
7 'Grandad' by Clive Dunn
8 'Ernie, the Fastest Milkman in the West' by Benny Hill
9 'Bright Eyes' by Art Garfunkel
10 'There's No One Quite like Grandma' by St Winifred's School Choir

Favourite television programmes

Beaver survey

1 *Buck Rogers in the 25th Century*
2 *The Professionals*
3 *Grange Hill*
4 *Hammer House of Horror*
5 *Not the Nine O'Clock News* and *Dr Who*
6 *Dallas* and *Blue Peter*
7 *The Dukes of Hazzard*
8 *Starsky and Hutch* and *The Muppets*
9 *Match of the Day, Tiswas, Top of the Pops* and *Battlestar Galactica*
10 *Charlie's Angels*

A January 1980 survey asked children to name their favourites from a list of television programmes.

Carrick James Market Research survey for Wall's Ice-Cream Limited

Fawlty Towers	23 per cent
Top of the Pops	19 per cent
Incredible Hulk	11 per cent
Charlie's Angels	8 per cent
Star Trek	7 per cent
Jim'll Fix It	7 per cent
Blue Peter	4 per cent
Dr Who	4 per cent
Take Hart	4 per cent
others	13 per cent

and two months later, the overall favourites across a wide age range were *Dallas*, *Top of the Pops* and 'cartoons'.

The two previous lists contain a number of programmes which are, in theory, adult shows. Now for the programmes made specially for children. A survey of the most popular children's programmes carried out by the Independent Broadcasting Authority found the following favourites:

1 *Crackerjack*
2 *The Adventures of Morph*
3 *Blue Peter*
4 *Jana of the Jungle*
5 *Mighty Mouse*
6 *Grandad*
7 *The Record Breakers*
8 *Buck Rogers in the 25th Century*
9 *Grange Hill*
10 *Worzel Gummidge*

Favourite books

Beaver survey

1 *Charlie and the Chocolate Factory*
2 Famous Five stories and Willard Price adventures
3 *Watership Down*
4 *Star Wars*
5 James Bond books and *The Empire Strikes Back*
6 *The Magic Faraway Tree* and *The Lion, the Witch and the Wardrobe*
7 *The Hobbit* and *Jaws*
8 Winnie the Pooh books and the Sherlock Holmes stories, especially *Hound of the Baskervilles*
   equal in ninth place:
   The Ogre Downstairs
   Jack and the Beanstalk
   Charlie and the Great Glass Elevator
   Rupert Bear books
   The Silver Sword
   Swallows and Amazons books
   Beatrix Potter books

and there were too many who came tenth to list them!

Favourite authors

Beaver survey

1 Enid Blyton
2 Roald Dahl
3 Robert Arthur
4 Willard Price
5 Michael Bond
6 Ian Fleming
7 Agatha Christie
   equal in eighth place:
   Charles Dickens
   Dorothy Edwards

Jane Fisher
J. R. R. Tolkein
Noel Streatfeild
equal in ninth place:
Alistair Maclean and Beatrix Potter
equal in tenth place:
Arthur C. Clarke
Franklin W. Dixon
Michael Hardcastle
Roger Hargreaves
James Herbert
Carolyne Keen
George Lucas
Arthur Ransome

Best-selling children's books 1980

Compiled from the best-seller lists the National Book League
has done for *The Bookseller* during the year.

1 *Grange Hill Rules OK?* by Robert Leeson (Fontana)
2 *Gentleman Jim* by Raymond Briggs (Hamish Hamilton)
3 *The Blue Peter Book of Gorgeous Grub* edited by Biddy
    Baxter (Piccolo)
4 *Brambly Hedge* (4 titles) by Jill Barklem (Collins)
5 *The Old Man of Lochnagar* by H R H The Prince of Wales
    (Hamish Hamilton)
6 *The Snowman* by Raymond Briggs (Puffin)
7 *Asterix in Belgium* by René Goscinny (Hodder and
    Stoughton)
8 *Captain Beaky* by Jeremy Lloyd (Elm Tree)
9 *Busy Town Pop-up Book* by Richard Scarry (Collins)
10 *The End* by Richard Stanley (Puffin)

Favourite comics and magazines

1 *Beano*
2 *Whizzer & Chips*
3 *Jackie*
4 *Roy of the Rovers*
5 *Shoot!*
6 *My Guy* and *Jackpot*
7 *Dandy*
8 *Whoopee*
9 *Nutty*
10 *Match Weekly*

Beano was five times as popular as the next comic on the list. Wow!

And what the publishers say. . . .

IPC Youth Magazines Group, which publishes many of the children's magazines and comics, recently reported their best-selling titles. Young children's favourites were *Fun To Do*, *Jack and Jill* and *Playhour*; most popular 'funnies' were *Buster*, *Jackpot, Mickey Mouse, Whizzer & Chips* and *Whoopee!*; girls' favourites were *Tammy* and *Jinty*; and the best-selling adventure titles were *Battle/Action, Tiger, Roy of the Rovers* and *2000 A D*. Their complete list of the top twenty best-sellers is as follows:

Battle/Action
Buster
Fab Hits
Fun To Do
Jack & Jill
Jackpot
Jinty
Look & Learn

Mates
Mickey Mouse
My Guy
Oh Boy!
Photo-Love
Playhour
Roy of the Rovers
Shoot!
Soccer Monthly
Tammy
Tiger
2000 AD

D. C. Thomson's, publishers of many popular comics, report that sales of *Beano* are way ahead of all the other young children's comics, followed in popularity by *Dandy* and *Topper*. However, *Jackie*, a teenage magazine, sells even better than *Beano*. So there.

10 Sport

Bookshelves, and diaries, are full of sporting facts and figures, so we haven't tried to compete with the many existing sporting record books. Instead, some opinions produced by our survey, and a few interesting and unusual lists about some of the more popular sports.

Favourite football player

According to the by now very famous Beaver survey, these are children's favourite footballers.

1 Kevin Keegan
2 Kenny Dalglish
3 Andy Gray
4 Danny McGrain
5 Cyril Regis, Gordon Cowans, Vince Hilaire and Glen Hoddle
6 Clive Walker

Kevin Keegan was twice as popular as Kenny Dalglish. Places 7 to 10 on the list were equally shared by too many players to list!

Favourite sport

Some more favourites from the Beaver survey.

1 football
2 swimming
3 netball
4 tennis and rugby
5 cricket and running
6 hockey
7 athletics
8 badminton and riding
9 ice-skating
10 show jumping, gymnastics, basketball and judo

Football was twice as popular as swimming.

Footballers of the year

Elected annually since 1947–8 by the Football Writers' Association.

1947–8	Stanley Matthews
1948–9	Johnny Carey
1949–50	Joe Mercer
1950–51	Harry Johnston
1951–2	Billy Wright
1952–3	Nat Lofthouse
1953–4	Tom Finney
1954–5	Don Revie
1955–6	Bert Trautmann
1956–7	Tom Finney
1957–8	Danny Blanchflower
1958–9	Sid Owen

1959–60	Bill Slater
1960–61	Danny Blanchflower
1961–2	Jimmy Adamson
1962–3	Stanley Matthews
1963–4	Bobby Moore
1964–5	Bobby Collins
1965–6	Bobby Charlton
1966–7	Jackie Charlton
1967–8	George Best
1968–9	Dave Mackay and Tony Book
1969–70	Billy Bremner
1970–71	Frank McLintock
1971–2	Gordon Banks
1972–3	Pat Jennings
1973–4	Ian Callaghan
1974–5	Alan Mulley
1975–6	Kevin Keegan
1976–7	Emlyn Hughes
1977–8	Kenny Burns
1978–9	Kenny Dalglish
1979–80	Terry McDermott

Longest-serving footballers

These are the players in the history of English Football League who have played the most competitive games for the same club.

	games
John Trollope, Swindon	765
Jimmy Dickinson, Portsmouth	764
Roy Sproson, Port Vale	761
Terry Paine, Southampton	713
Ron Harris, Chelsea	641
Ian Callaghan, Liverpool	640
Jack Charlton, Leeds	629
Joe Shaw, Sheffield United	629

Jasper Carrott's favourite footballers

Mr Carrott is a Director of Birmingham City FC and a regular full-back for his local team, Hockley Heath Rangers. 'Not the obscure Hockley Heath Rangers. THE Hockley Heath Rangers.' These are his favourite British footballers, with comments.

1 **Malcolm Macdonald**, ex-Newcastle United and Arsenal. 'I like him as a player and as a person.'

2 **Trevor Francis**, Nottingham Forest. 'Britain's most skilful player.'

3 **Gary Pendrey**, West Bromwich Albion. 'He's your bog standard ace, a Club prop. Without him, football would not exist.'

4 **Stanley Matthews**, ex-Blackpool. 'I've had my photograph taken with him, haven't I? That was a great ambition achieved.'

5 **Joe Mercer**, ex-Arsenal. 'He's the England team's most successful manager. He didn't lose a match – and he's one of the nicest people I've met.'

6 **Eddie Brown**, ex-Birmingham City. 'I used to watch him as a boy. He was a real clown. He used to shake hands with policemen and corner flags.'

7 **Jimmy Greaves**, ex-Tottenham Hotspur. 'Apart from his obvious goal-scoring feats, I think the way he's come through his tragedy since then (his alcoholism) with such dignity is an example to us all.'

Nicknames of well-known British clubs

Aberdeen	'Dons'
Arsenal	'Gunners'
Aston Villa	'Villans'
Birmingham City	'Blues'
Blackburn Rovers	'Rovers' or 'Blue & Whites'
Bolton	'Trotters'
Brighton	'Seagulls'
Bristol City	'Robins'
Bristol Rovers	'Pirates'

Burnley	'Clarets'
Cardiff City	'Bluebirds'
Celtic	'Bhoys'
Charlton	'Haddicks', 'Robins' or 'Valiants'
Chelsea	'Blues'
Coventry	'Sky Blues'
Crystal Palace	'Eagles'
Derby County	'Rams'
Dundee United	'Terrors'
Everton	'Toffeemen' or 'Blues'
Fulham	'Cottagers'
Heart of Midlothian	'Hearts'
Hibernian	'Hibs'
Ipswich	'Town'
Leeds United	'Peacocks'
Leicester City	'Filberts' or 'Foxes' or 'City'
Liverpool	'Reds' or 'Pool'
Luton Town	'Hatters'
Manchester City	'Citizens' or 'City'
Manchester United	'Red Devils'
Middlesbrough	'Boro'
Millwall	'Lions'
Morton	'Ton'
Motherwell	'Well'
Newcastle United	'Magpies'
Norwich City	'Canaries'
Nottingham Forest	'Reds'
Notts County	'Magpies'
Oldham	'Latics'
Orient	'O's'
Partick Thistle	'Jags'
Preston North End	'Lillywhites' or 'North End'
Queens Park Rangers	'Rangers' or 'R's'
Rangers	'Blues' or 'Gers'
Sheffield United	'Blades'
Sheffield Wednesday	'Owls'
Southampton	'Saints'
St Mirren	'Buddies'

Stoke City	'Potters'
Sunderland	'Rokerites'
Tottenham Hotspur	'Spurs'
West Bromwich Albion	'Throstles' or 'Albion'
West Ham United	'Hammers' or 'Irons'
Wolverhampton Wanderers	'Wolves'
Wrexham	'Robins'

Football crowds, 1979–80

Jake Davies, using all his fingers, has been taking a look at attendance figures at last season's First Division League matches. These are the top ten teams, with their total and their average attendances, based on home and away games.

		total attendance for all League matches	average attendance for all matches
1	Manchester United	1 797 950	42 808
2	Liverpool	1 677 411	39 938
3	Manchester City	1 305 848	31 092
4	Tottenham Hotspur	1 280 587	30 490
5	Arsenal	1 269 746	30 232
6	Nottingham Forest	1 184 498	28 202
7	Crystal Palace	1 171 946	27 903
8	Aston Villa	1 143 170	27 218
9	Everton	1 129 052	26 882
10	Wolverhampton Wanderers	1 105 977	26 333

Football: the hat-trick men

Nicholas Mason, Deputy Sports Editor of *The Sunday Times*, has painstakingly compiled this and the rest of the football lists. Sixty-one hat-tricks (three goals by an individual in one match) have been scored by England footballers in internationals since 1872; thirty-two have been scored by Scotland footballers; ten for Wales and six for Northern Ireland (known as Ireland up to 1946).

Twelve men have scored more than one hat-trick for one or other of the Home countries in international football. They are:

Six times: JIMMY GREAVES (England) (1960–66)
Four times: V. J. WOODWARD (England) (1908–9)
               BOBBY CHARLTON (England) (1959–63)
Three times: R. S. MCCOLL (Scotland) (1899–1900)
               HUGHIE GALLACHER (Scotland) (1926–9)
               STANLEY MORTENSEN (England) (1947–8)
               DENIS LAW (Scotland) (1962–3)
Twice: STEVE BLOOMER (England) (1896–1901)
               R. C. HAMILTON (Scotland) (1901–2)
               'DIXIE' DEAN (England) (1927)
               GEORGE CAMSELL (England) (1929)
               TOMMY LAWTON (England) (1946–7)

The hat-trick plus men

On thirty-seven occasions, a player has scored four goals or more in a match for one of the Home countries. They are:

For England (21)
O. H. VAUGHTON (5 goals) v Ireland, 1882
A. BROWN (4) v Ireland, 1882
B. W. SPILSBURY (4) v Ireland, 1886
S. BLOOMER (5) v Wales, 1896
G. O. SMITH (4) v Ireland, 1899
S. BLOOMER (4) v Wales, 1901
V. J. WOODWARD (4) v Austria, 1908
G. R. HILSDON (4) v Hungary, 1908
V. J. WOODWARD (4) v Hungary, 1909
G. H. CAMSELL (4) v Belgium, 1929
G. W. HALL (5) v Ireland, 1938
T. LAWTON (4) v Netherlands, 1946
T. LAWTON (4) v Portugal, 1947

S. MORTENSEN (4) v Portugal, 1947
J. F. ROWLEY (4) v N. Ireland, 1949
T. FINNEY (4) v Portugal, 1950
D. J. WILSHAW (4) v Scotland, 1955
J. GREAVES (4) v N. Ireland, 1963
R. HUNT (4) v USA, 1964
J. GREAVES (4) v Norway, 1966
M. MACDONALD (5) v Cyprus, 1975

For Scotland (12)
A. HIGGINS (4) v Ireland, 1885
C. HEGGIE (5) v Ireland, 1886
W. PAUL (4) v Wales, 1890
J. MADDEN (4) v Wales, 1893
A. MCMAHON (4) v Ireland, 1901
R. C. HAMILTON (4) v Ireland, 1901
J. QUINN (4) v Ireland, 1908
H. K. GALLACHER (4) v Wales, 1928
W. STEEL (4) v N. Ireland, 1950
D. LAW (4) v N. Ireland, 1962
D. LAW (4) v Norway, 1963
C. STEIN (4) v Cyprus, 1969

For Wales (4)
J. PRICE (4) v Ireland, 1882
J. DOUGHTY (4) v Ireland, 1888
M. CHARLES (4) v N. Ireland, 1962
R. I. EDWARDS (4) v Malta, 1978

No Northern Ireland player has scored more than three goals
in an international match.

Cup specialists

Up to 1980, thirty clubs, some of them now extinct, had
reached the FA Cup Final on three occasions or more:

11   Newcastle United (6 wins)
     Arsenal (5 wins)

10   West Bromwich Albion (5 wins)
 9   Aston Villa (7 wins)
 8   Blackburn Rovers (6 wins)
     Manchester United (4 wins)
     Wolverhampton Wanderers (4 wins)
 7   Bolton Wanderers (4 wins)
     Preston North End (2 wins)
     Everton (3 wins)
     Manchester City (4 wins)
 6   Liverpool (2 wins)
     Old Etonians (2 wins)
     Sheffield United (4 wins)
 5   Huddersfield Town (1 win)
     The Wanderers (5 wins)
     Sheffield Wednesday (3 wins)
     Tottenham Hotspur (5 wins)
 4   West Ham United (3 wins)
     Derby County (1 win)
     Oxford University (1 win)
     Royal Engineers (1 win)
     Leeds United (1 win)
     Leicester City (no wins)
 3   Blackpool (1 win)
     Burnley (1 win)
     Chelsea (1 win)
     Portsmouth (1 win)
     Sunderland (2 wins)
     Southampton (1 win)

Worst Cup sides

Football League teams which have recorded least progress over the history of the FA Cup.

Never beyond the Fourth Round
Cambridge United
Hartlepool United
Hereford United

Rochdale
Torquay United
Wigan Athletic
Wimbledon

Never beyond the Fifth Round
Aldershot
Brighton & Hove Albion
Chester
Chesterfield
Darlington
Doncaster Rovers
Gillingham
Halifax Town
Lincoln City
Newport County
Northampton Town
Plymouth Argyle
Rotherham United
Scunthorpe United
Southend United
Stockport County
Tranmere Rovers
Walsall

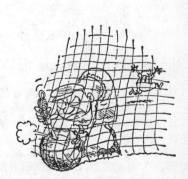

Phew, so that's the football finished. Now let's look at some
other sports.

Show jumping

Leading Show Jumper of the Year

1960	Ted Williams on Pegasus XIII
1961	Tied: D. B. Barker on Lucky Sam
	Miss C. Beard on Mayfly
1962	Miss Pat Smythe on Flanagan
1963	A. Fielder on Vibart
1964	Mrs C. D. Barker on Atalanta
1965	Harvey Smith on Warpaint

1966	A. Fielder on Vibart
1967	Harvey Smith on Harvester VI
1968	A. Fielder on Vibart
1969	Ted Edgar on Uncle Max
1970	Mrs Marion Mould (née Coakes) on Stroller
1971	Alan Oliver on Pitz Palu
1972	Miss Ann Moore on Psalm
1973	David Broome on Sportsman
1974	Graham Fletcher on Tauna Dora
1975	David Broome on Sportsman
1976	Miss Debbie Johnsey on Speculator
1977	Miss Caroline Bradley on Marius
1978	Nick Skelton on Maybe
1979	Robert Smith on Video
1980	Malcolm Pyrah on Towerlands Anglezarke

Junior Show Jumper of the Year

1960	Tied: Miss J. Goodwin on Carreg Guest
	Miss A. Westwood on Lulu
1961	Tied: Miss P. Langton on Mister Robin
	D. Hughes on Carreg Guest
1962	Miss C. Inskip on Grey Mist VIII
1963	Miss G. M. Cambridge on Little Robert
1964	Miss L. Raper on Pierrot
1965	Miss L. Raper on Pierrot
1966	Miss N. Loffett on Kangaroo
1967	Miss N. Loffett on Kangaroo
1968	M. Hall Hall on Pablo
1969	J. Simms on Ki-Ming
1970	Miss J. M. Tempest on Jenny Wren IX
1971	Miss P. Wilson on Court Colando
1972	Miss S. Pitcher on Pim III
1973	G. Gillespie on Starlight XLII
1974	Miss D. Saffell on Lockwood Cedric
1975	J. Webb on Ivanhoe XI
1976	Michael Whitaker on Tamarisk II
1977	Michael Mac on Dunglenn VII
1978	K. Fuller on Telstar XXI

1979   Miss Carolyn Thomas on Rival II
1980   Miss Marnie Wilson on The Welshman

Motor racing

World champion drivers

1950   Giuseppe Farina (Italy), Alfa Romeo
1951   Juan-Manuel Fangio (Argentina), Alfa Romeo
1952   Alberto Ascari (Italy), Ferrari
1953   Alberto Ascari (Italy), Ferrari
1954   Juan-Manuel Fangio (Argentina), Maserati and
       Mercedes-Benz
1955   Juan-Manuel Fangio (Argentina), Mercedes-Benz
1956   Juan-Manuel Fangio (Argentina), Ferrari
1957   Juan-Manuel Fangio (Argentina), Maserati
1958   J. M. (Mike) Hawthorn (Great Britain), Ferrari
1959   Jack Brabham (Australia), Cooper
1960   Jack Brabham (Australia), Cooper
1961   Phil Hill (USA), Ferrari
1962   Graham Hill (Great Britain), B.R.M.
1963   Jim Clark (Great Britain), Lotus
1964   John Surtees (Great Britain), Ferrari
1965   Jim Clark (Great Britain), Lotus
1966   Jack Brabham (Australia), Brabham
1967   Denis Hulme (New Zealand), Brabham
1968   Graham Hill (Great Britain), Lotus
1969   Jackie Stewart (Great Britain), Matra
1970   Jochen Rindt (Austria), Lotus
1971   Jackie Stewart (Great Britain), Tyrrell
1972   Emerson Fittlpaldi (Brazil), Lotus
1973   Jackie Stewart (Great Britain), Tyrrell
1974   Emerson Fittipaldi (Brazil), McLaren
1975   Niki Lauda (Austria), Ferrari
1976   James Hunt (Great Britain), McLaren Ford
1977   Niki Lauda (Austria), Ferrari
1978   Mario Andretti (USA), Lotus
1979   Jody Scheckter (South Africa), Ferrari
1980   Alan Jones (Australia), Williams

Grand prix

First run as the RAC Grand Prix at Brooklands in 1926, the name British Grand Prix was first used in 1949. This is a full list of winners, circuits, and distance. No sign of Mark Thatcher so far....

	driver	car	circuit	distance (miles)	speed (mph)
1926	Robert Senechal/Louis Wagner	Delage	Brooklands	287	71·61
1927	Robert Benoist	Delage	Brooklands	325	85·59
*1935	Richard Shuttleworth	Alfa Romeo	Donington	306	63·97
1936	Hans Ruesch/Richard Seaman	Alfa Romeo	Donington	306	69·23
1937	Bernd Rosemeyer	Auto-Union	Donington	250	82·85
1938	Tazio Nuvolari	Auto-Union	Donington	250	80·49
1948	Luigi Villoresi	Maserati	Silverstone	250	72·28
1949	Baron Emmanuel de Graffenried	Maserati	Silverstone	300	77·31
1950	Giuseppe Farina	Alfa Romeo	Silverstone	202	90·95
1951	Froilan Gonzalez	Ferrari	Silverstone	253	96·11
1952	Alberto Ascari	Ferrari	Silverstone	249	90·92
1953	Alberto Ascari	Ferrari	Silverstone	263	92·97
1954	Froilan Gonzalez	Ferrari	Silverstone	270	89·69
*1955	Stirling Moss	Mercedes-Benz	Aintree	270	86·47
1956	Juan Manuel Fangio	Ferrari	Silverstone	300	98·65
*1957	Tony Brooks/Stirling Moss	Vanwall	Aintree	270	86·80
*1958	Peter Collins	Ferrari	Silverstone	225	102·05

1959	Jack Brabham	Cooper-Climax	Aintree	225	89·88
1960	Jack Brabham	Cooper-Climax	Silverstone	231	108·69
1961	Wolfgang von Trips	Ferrari	Aintree	225	83·91
*1962	Jim Clark	Lotus-Climax	Aintree	225	92·25
*1963	Jim Clark	Lotus-Climax	Silverstone	246	107·75
*1964	Jim Clark	Lotus-Climax	Brands Hatch	212	94·14
*1965	Jim Clark	Lotus-Climax	Silverstone	240	112·02
1966	Jack Brabham	Repco Brabham	Brands Hatch	212	95·48
*1967	Jim Clark	Lotus-Ford	Silverstone	240	117·64
1968	Joseph Siffert	Lotus-Ford	Brands Hatch	212	104·83
*1969	Jackie Stewart	Matra-Ford	Silverstone	246	127·25
1970	Jochen Rindt	Lotus-Ford	Brands Hatch	212	108·69
*1971	Jackie Stewart	Tyrrell-Ford	Silverstone	199	130·48
1972	Emerson Fittipaldi	JPS-Ford	Brands Hatch	201	112·06
1973	Peter Revson	McLaren-Ford	Silverstone	196	131·75
1974	Jody Scheckter	Tyrrell-Ford	Brands Hatch	199	115·73
1975	Emerson Fittipaldi	McLaren-Ford	Silverstone	164	120·01
1976	Niki Lauda	Ferrari	Brands Hatch	198	114·24
*1977	James Hunt	McLaren-Ford	Silverstone	199	130·36
1978	Carlos Reutemann	Ferrari	Brands Hatch	199	116·61
1979	'Clay' Regazzoni	Saudia-Williams	Silverstone	199	138·80
1980	Alan Jones	Saudia-Leyland-Williams	Brands Hatch	199	125·69

* British winners

Athletics

Olympic Gold Medals won by British athletes since the modern games began in 1896. Over the years the USA has won the greatest number of medals for athletics.

1896   none
1900   Alfred Tysoe (800 metres), Charles Bennett (1 500 metres)
1904   none
1908   Wyndham Halswell (400 metres), Timothy Ahearne (triple jump)
1912   Arnold Jackson (1 500 metres), 4 × 100 metres relay team (David Jacobs, Harold Macintosh, Victor d'Arcy and William Applegarth)
1920   Albert Hill (800 metres), Albert Hill (1 500 metres), Percy Hodge (3 000 metres steeplechase), 4 × 400 metres relay team (Cecil Griffiths, Robert Lindsay, John Ainsworth-David, Guy Butler)
1924   Harold Abrahams (100 metres), Eric Liddell (400 metres), Douglas Lowe (800 metres)
1928   Douglas Lowe (800 metres) Lord Burghley (400 metres hurdles)
1932   Thomas Hampson (800 metres), Thomas Green (50 000 metres walk)
1936   4 × 400 metres relay team (Frederick Wolff, Godfrey Rampling, William Roberts, Godfrey Brown), Harold Whitlock (50 000 metres walk)
1948   none
1952   none
1956   Christopher Brasher (3 000 metres steeplechase)
1964   Ken Matthews (20 000 metres walk), Lynn Davies (long jump), Ann Packer (women's 800 metres), Mary Rand (women's long jump)
1968   David Hemery (400 metres hurdles)
1972   Mary Peters (women's pentathlon)
1976   none
1980   Daley Thompson (decathlon), Sebastian Coe (1 500 metres), Steve Ovett (800 metres), Alan Wells (100 metres)

Cricket

Not content with dazzling us with his football facts, Nicholas Mason now looks at cricket. Well played, Nick.

All-round performance at Test Match level

Players who have scored 1000 runs and taken 100 wickets in Tests for England (figures correct to 1 January 1981).

player	tests	runs	wickets	test in which double was achieved
I. T. Botham	31	1505	153	21st
M. W. Tate	39	1198	155	33rd
A. W. Greig	58	3599	141	37th
F. J. Titmus	53	1449	153	40th
W. Rhodes	58	2325	127	44th
T. E. Bailey	61	2290	132	47th
R. Illingworth	61	1836	122	47th

Full list of hat-tricks
(three wickets in consecutive balls) taken in Test Matches for England

W. BATES v Australia (Melbourne, 1882-3)

J. BRIGGS v Australia (Sydney, 1891-2)

G. A. LOHMANN v South Africa (Port Elizabeth, 1895-6)

J. T. HEARNE v Australia (Leeds, 1899)

M. J. C. ALLOM v New Zealand (Christchurch, 1929-30)

T. W. J. GODDARD v South Africa (Johannesburg, 1938-9)

P. J. LOADER v West Indies (Leeds, 1957)

Highest total for each of the first-class counties

Derbyshire	645	v Hampshire (Derby, 1898)
Essex	692	v Somerset (Taunton, 1895)
Glamorgan	587 (8 wkts)	v Derbyshire (Cardiff, 1951)
Gloucestershire	653 (6 wkts)	v Glamorgan (Bristol, 1928)

Hampshire	672 (7 wkts)	v Somerset (Taunton, 1899)
Kent	803 (4 wkts)	v Essex (Brentwood, 1934)
Lancashire	801	v Somerset (Taunton, 1895)
Leicestershire	701 (4 wkts)	v Worcestershire (Worcester, 1906)
Middlesex	642 (3 wkts)	v Hampshire (Southampton, 1923)
Northamptonshire	557 (6 wkts)	v Sussex (Hove, 1914)
Nottinghamshire	739 (7 wkts)	v Leicestershire (Nottingham, 1903)
Somerset	675 (9 wkts)	v Hampshire (Bath, 1924)
Surrey	811	v Somerset (Oval, 1899)
Sussex	705 (8 wkts)	v Surrey (Hastings, 1902)
Warwickshire	657 (6 wkts)	v Hampshire (Birmingham, 1899)
Worcestershire	633	v Warwickshire (Worcester, 1906)
Yorkshire	887	v Warwickshire (Birmingham, 1896)

Lowest total by each first-class county

Derbyshire	16	v Nottinghamshire (Nottingham, 1879)
Essex	30	v Yorkshire (Leyton, 1901)
Glamorgan	22	v Lancashire (Liverpool, 1924)
Gloucestershire	17	v Australia (Cheltenham, 1896)
Hampshire	15	v Warwickshire (Birmingham, 1922)
Kent	18	v Sussex (Gravesend, 1867)
Lancashire	25	v Derbyshire (Manchester, 1871)
Leicestershire	25	v Kent (Leicester, 1912)
Middlesex	20	v MCC (Lord's, 1864)
Northamptonshire	12	v Gloucestershire (Gloucester, 1907)
Nottinghamshire	13	v Yorkshire (Nottingham, 1901)
Somerset	25	v Gloucestershire (Bristol, 1947)
Surrey	16	v Nottinghamshire (Oval, 1880)
Sussex	19	v Nottinghamshire (Hove, 1873)
Warwickshire	16	v Kent (Tonbridge, 1913)
Worcestershire	24	v Yorkshire (Huddersfield, 1903)
Yorkshire	23	v Hampshire (Middlesbrough, 1965)

A full list of the success records of all the players who have captained England in Test Matches since the war
(To the end of 1980)

The Wisden Book of Test Cricket

name	won	lost	drawn
W. R. Hammond	1	3	5 (pre-war: 3–0–8)
N. W. D. Yardley	4	7	3

K. Cranston	0	0	1
F. G. Mann	2	0	5
F. R. Brown	5	6	4
N. D. Howard	1	0	3
D. B. Carr	0	1	0
L. Hutton	11	4	8
D. S. Sheppard	1	0	1
P. B. H. May	20	10	11
M. C. Cowdrey	8	4	15
E. R. Dexter	9	7	14
M. J. K. Smith	5	3	17
D. B. Close	6	0	1
T. W. Graveney	0	0	1
R. Illingworth	12	5	14
A. R. Lewis	1	2	5
M. H. Denness	6	5	8
J. H. Edrich	0	1	0
A. W. Greig	3	5	6
J. M. Brearley	15	4	7
G. Boycott	1	1	2
I. T. Botham	0	1	5

Youngest players to represent their country in a Test Match

Age shown on the first day of their first Test

15 years 124 days – Mushtaq Mohammad (Pakistan v West Indies, 1958–9)

16 years 191 days – Aftab Baloch (Pakistan v New Zealand, 1969–70)

16 years 248 days – Nasim-Ul-Ghani (Pakistan v West Indies, 1957–8)

16 years 352 days – Khalid Hassan (Pakistan v England, 1954)

17 years 122 days – J. E. D. Sealy (West Indies v England, 1929–30)

17 years 239 days – I. D. Craig (Australia v South Africa, 1952–3)

17 years 245 days – G. St. A. Sobers (West Indies v England, 1953–4)

17 years 265 days – V. L. Mehra (India v New Zealand, 1955–6)

17 years 300 days – Hanif Mohammad (Pakistan v India (1952–3)

17 years 341 days – Intikhab Alam (Pakistan v Australia, 1959–60)

18 years 26 days – Majid Kahn (Pakistan v Australia, 1964–5)

18 years 31 days – M. R. Bynoe (West Indies v Pakistan, 1958–9)

18 years 41 days – Salahuddin (Pakistan v New Zealand, 1964–5)

18 years 44 days – Khalid Wazir (Pakistan v England, 1954)

18 years 105 days – J. B. Stollmeyer (West Indies v England, 1939)

18 years 149 days – D. B. Close (England v New Zealand, 1949)

Olympic Games

Total number of medals won at summer Olympic Games 1896–1980

International Olympic Committee archives

USA	1514½	Switzerland	158
Russia	865	Denmark	142½
UK	547½	Netherlands	136
W. Germany	494½	Belgium	127
France	463	Canada	122
Sweden	413	Norway	101
Italy	360	Austria	83
E. Germany	306	Spain	17
Japan	200	Ireland	13
Australia	187		

½ = tie with other country.

Winter sports : British medal winners

Britain has won only fifteen individual or team medals in the

Winter Olympic Games since the first Winter Games in 1908.
The winners were:

gold
1936 Ice hockey team
1952 Jeanette Altwegg (figure skating, women)
1964 Two-man bobsleigh team (Tony Nash, Robin Dixon)
1976 John Curry (figure skating, men)
1980 Robin Cousins (figure skating, men)
silver
1908 Phyllis and James Johnson (figure skating, pairs)
1936 Cecilia Colledge (figure skating, women)
bronze
1908 Dorothy Greenhough-Smith (figure skating, women)
1908 Madge and Edgar Syers (figure skating, pairs)
1924 Ethel Muckelt (figure skating, women)
1924 Ice hockey team
1928 Lord Northesk (skeleton toboggan)
1936 Four man bobsleigh team (F. McEvoy, J. Cardno,
         G. Dugdale, C. Green)
1948 Jeanette Altwegg (figure skating, women)
1948 John Crammond (skeleton toboggan)

Motorcycle racing

500cc motorcycle road racing world champions

1970 Giacomo Agostini (Italy, MV Agusta)
1971 Giacomo Agostini (Italy, MV Agusta)
1972 Giacomo Agostini (Italy, MV Agusta)
1973 Phil Read (GB, MV Agusta)
1974 Phil Read (GB, MV Agusta)
1975 Giacomo Agostini (Italy, Yamaha)
1976 Barry Sheene (GB, Suzuki)
1977 Barry Sheene (GB, Suzuki)
1978 Kenny Roberts (USA, Yamaha)
1979 Kenny Roberts (USA, Yamaha)
1980 Kenny Roberts (USA, Yamaha)

World speedway champions

1970 Ivan Mauger (New Zealand)
1971 Ole Olsen (Denmark)
1972 Ivan Mauger (New Zealand)
1973 Jerzy Szczakiel (Poland)
1974 Anders Michanek (Sweden)
1975 Ole Olsen (Denmark)
1976 Peter Collins (GB)
1977 Ivan Mauger (New Zealand)
1978 Ole Olsen (Denmark)
1979 Ivan Mauger (New Zealand)
1980 Michael Lee (GB)

500cc motocross world champions

1970 Bengt Aberg (Sweden)
1971 Roger de Coster (Belgium)
1972 Roger de Coster (Belgium)
1973 Roger de Coster (Belgium)
1974 Heikki Mikkola (Finland)
1975 Roger de Coster (Belgium)
1976 Roger de Coster (Belgium)
1977 Heikki Mikkola (Finland)
1978 Heikki Mikkola (Finland)
1979 Graham Noyce (GB)
1980 Andre Malherbe (Belgium)

World motorcycle trials champions

1970 Sammy Miller (GB)
1971 Mick Andrews (GB)
1972 Mick Andrews (GB)
1973 Martin Lampkin (GB)
1974 Martin Rathmell (GB)
1975 Martin Lampkin (GB)
1976 Yrjo Vesterinen (Finland)
1977 Yrjo Vesterinen (Finland)
1978 Yrjo Vesterinen (Finland)
1979 Bernie Schreiber (USA)
1980 Ulf Karlsson (Sweden)

Tennis

Youngest Wimbledon winners

Lawn Tennis Association

girls
1 1887   C. Dodd aged 15
2 1952   Maureen Connolly aged 17
3 1971   Evonne Goolagong (now Cawley) aged 19
   1974   Chris Evert (now Evert-Lloyd) aged 19
4 1963   Margaret Smith (now Court) aged 20

boys
1 1931   S. B. Wood aged 19
2 1976   Bjorn Borg aged 20
3 1925   René Lacoste aged 21
   1939   Bobby Riggs aged 21
   1956   Lew Hoad aged 21
   1958   H. Cooper aged 21

The BBC Sports Personality of the Year

Each year viewers of *Grandstand* and other BBC television sports programmes cast their votes to find the year's outstanding sports personality. These are the winners since the competition began:

1954   Christopher Chataway (athletics)
1955   Gordon Pirie (athletics)
1956   Jim Laker (cricket)
1957   Dai Rees (golf)
1958   Ian Black (swimming)
1959   John Surtees (motor cycling)
1960   David Broome (show jumping)
1961   Stirling Moss (motor racing)
1962   Anita Lonsborough (swimming)

1963	Dorothy Hyman (athletics)
1964	Mary Rand (athletics)
1965	Tommy Simpson (cycling)
1966	Bobby Moore (football)
1967	Henry Cooper (boxing)
1968	David Hemery (athletics)
1969	Ann Jones (tennis)
1970	Henry Cooper (boxing)
1971	Princess Anne (show jumping)
1972	Mary Peters (athletics)
1973	Jackie Stewart (motor racing)
1974	Brendan Foster (athletics)
1975	David Steele (cricket)
1976	John Curry (ice skating)
1977	Virginia Wade (tennis)
1978	Steve Ovett (athletics)
1979	Sebastian Coe (athletics)
1980	Robin Cousins (ice skating)

11 Names & Words

As a change from dates and numbers, here are a few names. And a few words. And also some names which are words.

Christian names

Margaret Brown of York has analysed the births announcements in *The Times* and provided a list of the most popular names.

Top people's names, 1980

For the seventeenth year in succession, James was the name most frequently chosen by readers announcing the birth of their sons in *The Times*. Elizabeth remained, throughout the Queen Mother's eightieth birthday year, the most popular name for girls.

(The figures in parentheses indicate the positions held during 1979.)

	boys		*girls*	
1	James	243 (1)	Elizabeth	148 (1)

2 Alexander	153 (6)	Louise	132 (8)
3 William	150 (7)	Jane	90 (3)
4 Thomas	136 (3)	Mary	75 (5)
5 John	135 (6)	Sarah	69 (2)
6 Edward	126 (2)	Alice	68 (11)
7 Charles	113 (8)	Clare	66 (6)
8 David	91 (9)	Victoria	66 (3)
9 Robert	78 (12)	Katherine	63 (18)
10 Richard	75 (10)	Alexandra	55 (14)

Eight of the ten boys' names have remained the same since 1978.

Surnames

The most common surnames in England and Wales

This is a traditional list, reproduced in several books, but accepted by most people as fairly accurate. Complete accuracy would be difficult to achieve, with almost 50 million names to count. . . .

1 Smith
2 Jones
3 Williams
4 Brown
5 Taylor
6 Davies
7 Evans
8 Thomas
9 Roberts
10 Johnson

Names which are numbers

Mr George Mell of Tadworth, Surrey, has amused himself for many years by compiling a list of place-names which are also numbers. This is his total so far. He's got names for each number up to twenty, but then, alas, he has a few gaps.

One Man's Pass, Co. Donegal, Eire.
Two Pots, Ilfracombe, Devon.
Three-Legged Cross, Dorset.
Four Throws, Kent.
Fivepenny Borve, Lewis, Hebrides.
Six Bells, Monmouthshire.
Seven Emu River, Australia.
Eightlands, Yorkshire.
Ninestane Rig, Roxburghshire.
Ten Acres, Birmingham.
Eleven Lane Ends, Co. Armagh, Northern Ireland.
Twelveheads, Cornwall.
Twelve Pins, Galway, Eire.
Baker's Dozen Islands, Hudson's Bay, Canada.
Fourteen Streams Station, South Africa.
Fifteen-Mile Falls Dam, Vermont, USA.
Sixteen Island Lake, Quebec, Canada.
Seventeen Mile Creek, Ontario, Canada.
Eighteen Mile Tank, New South Wales, Australia.
Nineteen Mile Creek, British Columbia, Canada.
Twenty, Lincolnshire.
Twenty-four Parganas, West Bengal, India.
Twenty Six, Kentucky, USA.
Twentynine Palms, Mojave Desert, California, USA.
Thirty-one Mile Lake, Quebec, Canada.
Treinta y Tres (Spanish for 33), Uruguay.
Trentanove (Italian for 39), Mediterranean islet.
Forty Foot Bridge, Huntingdonshire.
Eight and Forty, Yorkshire.
Fifty Six, Stone County, Arizona, USA
Sixty Mile River, Alaska.
Seventy Mile House, British Columbia, Canada.

Ninety Mile Beach, Victoria, Australia.
Ninety Six, South Carolina, USA.
Hundred House, Radnorshire, Wales.
Seven Score, Kent.
Thousand Oaks, California, USA.
Ten Thousand Smokes, Alaska.

He reports: 'My 1 to 20 sequence was destroyed in May 1968 when the Thirteen Arches railway viaduct, near Bristol, was blown up to make way for the M32, but I soon filled the gap with an acceptable 13 – Baker's Dozen Islands.

'Many numbers still elude me but I have lots of duplicates such as Three Bridges, Five Elms, Thousand Islands International Bridge (Ontario), Nine Mile Ride, Tenino (Washington, USA), Four Mile Bridge, Two Mile Hill, Sixmile Bridge (one in Northumberland and another in Co. Clare), Fifteen Arch Bridge, Forty Fork (Pennsylvania, USA), Ten Thousand Islands (Florida, USA), Six Towns (Londonderry) and several more.

'I'm still hoping to fill the many gaps in the above list.'

Previous names

People born with different names from the ones they later became famous with.

Josef Teodor Konrad Korzeniowski – Joseph Conrad
Archibald Leach – Cary Grant
Eric Arthur Blair – George Orwell
Richard Jenkins – Richard Burton
Barnet Winogradsky – Lord Delfont
Harry Webb – Cliff Richard
Reg Dwight – Elton John
Maurice Cole – Kenny Everett
Richard Starkey – Ringo Starr
Priscilla White – Cilla Black
Eric Bartholomew – Eric Morecambe
Cecily Isabel Fenwick – Dame Rebecca West

Lesley Hornby – Twiggy
Bob Davis – Jasper Carrott
Margaret Hookham – Margot Fonteyn
Alice Marks – Alicia Markova
Thomas Hicks – Tommy Steele
Maurice Micklewhite – Michael Caine
William Mitchell – Peter Finch
Michael Dumble-Smith – Michael Crawford

Unusual pub names

THE SNOOTY FOX: Tetbury, Gloucestershire
THE ELEPHANT'S NEST: Tavistock, Devon
THE BLUE MONKEY: Plymouth, Devon
THE CAT AND CUSTARD POT: Shipton Moyne, Wiltshire
THE DRUNKEN DUCK: Barngate, Cumbria
THE THREE PICKERELS: Mepal, Cambridgeshire
THE SILENT WHISTLE: Evercreech, Somerset
THE SILENT WOMAN: Cold Harbour, Dorset
THE HEADLESS WOMAN: Duddon, Cheshire
THE HONEST LAWYER: King's Lynn, Norfolk
THE CUCKOO BUSH: Gotham, Nottinghamshire
THE WALTZING WEASEL: Birch Vale, Hayfield, Derbyshire
DOFF COCKERS: Bolton, Lancashire
THE FINNEYGOOK: Crafthole, Cornwall
THE SCROGG: Newcastle upon Tyne
RHUBARB: Bristol
SACK OF POTATOES: Gosta Green, Birmingham
CUSTARD HOUSE: Small Heath, Birmingham
THE STORK AT REST: Stacey Close, Gravesend, Kent
THE STARVING RASCAL: Amblecote, West Midlands
BUNCH OF CARROTS: Hampton Bishop, Hereford
THE QUEEN'S HEAD AND ARTICHOKE: London

New words of the Seventies

Twenty new words which came into prominence in the
1970s, as selected by Dr R. W. Burchfield, chief editor of the
Oxford English dictionaries. Most of these words have

recently appeared in the various new editions of the Oxford dictionaries.

1 **Ayatollah,** a Muslim religious leader in Iran.

2 **Go bananas,** (slang) to go crazy.

3 **Bionic,** (of a person or his faculties) operated by electronic means, not naturally.

4 **Biorhythm,** any of the recurring cycles of physical, emotional and intellectual activity said to occur in people's lives.

5 **Eurodollar,** dollar held in bank in Europe etc., not in USA.

6 **Granny flat,** a flat in someone's house where an elderly relative can live independently but close to the family.

7 **Green pound,** the agreed value of the £ according to which payments to agricultural producers are reckoned in the EEC.

8 **Hatchback,** a car with a sloping back hinged at the top so that it can be opened; the back itself.

9 **Kneecapping,** shooting in the legs to lame a person as a punishment.

10 **Lassa fever,** acute febrile virus disease of tropical Africa.

11 **Minimum lending rate,** the announced minimum rate (influencing other rates of interest) at which the Bank of England lends or advances money.

12 **No-go area,** an area to which entry is forbidden to certain people or groups.

13 **Plea bargaining,** practice of agreeing to drop charge(s), or to sentence leniently, if the accused pleads guilty to other charge(s).

14 **Poverty trap,** the condition of being so dependent on State benefits that an increase in one's income merely means that one loses some of these and is no better off.

15 **Punk rock,** a type of pop music involving outrage and shock effects in music, behaviour and dress.

16 **Quadraphonic,** (of sound reproduction) using four transmission channels.

17 **Quango,** from the initials of quasi-autonomous non-governmental organisation.

18 **Secondary picketing,** picketing of a place other than one's own place of work during a trade union dispute.

19 **Shuttle diplomacy,** negotiations conducted by a mediator who travels to several countries at brief intervals.
20 **Skateboard,** a small board with wheels like those of roller-skates, for riding on (as a sport) while standing.

The ten most widely spoken languages in the world

1 Guoyu (standardised North Chinese) 700 000 000
2 English 375 000 000
3 Great Russian 250 000 000
4 Spanish 230 000 000
5 Hindustani 220 000 000
6 Bengali, Arabic and Portuguese 135 000 000 each
7 German 120 000 000
8 Japanese 110 000 000
9 Malay-Indonesian 100 000 000
10 French 95 000 000

Most popular foreign languages

Each week the Inner London Education Authority runs nearly 2000 classes in foreign languages at its various Adult Education Colleges throughout London. Judged by the number of classes laid on for each of the different languages, French is the most popular.

	classes per week		classes per week
French	594	Russian	32
German	348	Finnish	28
Spanish	294	Hebrew	28
Italian	230	Urdu	18
Bengalese	56	Portuguese	15
Greek	46	Japanese	13
Arabic	44	Turkish	13

Dutch	12	Swedish	8
Chinese	11	Welsh	5
Danish	10	Persian	4
Polish	10	Czech	3
Irish Gaelic	9	Bulgarian	3

Graffiti

Humpty Dumpty was pushed.

The grave of Karl Marx is just another communist plot.

God is not dead, but alive and well and working on a much
   less ambitious project.

Death is nature's way of telling you to slow down.

Prepare to meet thy God (evening dress optional).

Tolkein is hobbit-forming.

When God made man she was only testing.

Racial prejudice is a pigment of the imagination.

Nostalgia is not what it used to be.

Give me patience – now!

I love mankind – it's people I can't stand.

Insanity is hereditary – you get it from your children.

I hate graffiti – I hate all Italian food.

Save trees – eat a beaver.

Baby sitar wanted for young Indian musician.

Drink varnish – it gives a lovely finish.

Our needlework teacher is a so-and-so.

Mallet rules, croquet.

Eskimos are God's frozen people.

The upper crust are just a lot of crumbs sticking together.

Names which are words

Another of George Mell's compilations.

Boycott In 1880 Captain Charles C. Boycott, agent for a
number of Irish estates, refused to accept agreed figures for
rents. He was ignored by his neighbours, his life was threatened

and supplies of food were stopped in a campaign that brought the word 'boycott' into the English language. It means 'to shut out from all social and commercial intercourse'.

Cardigan This popular knitted waistcoat was named after the seventh Earl of Cardigan, who led the charge of the Light Brigade at Balaclava, and wore such a garment.

Gladstone This travelling bag was named after William Ewart Gladstone, British statesman. He did not invent it, but his name was applied to several articles popular during his lifetime (1809–98). This is the only one to remain in fairly general use.

Guillotine This instrument used for beheading criminals was not invented by the man after whom it is named – Joseph Ignace Guillotin. He was a French doctor who suggested its use on humanitarian grounds for the execution of highwaymen.

Macadam This word, meaning a smooth, hard road surface, is named after the man who introduced it – John Loudon Macadam (1756–1836).

Nicotine Jean Nicot, French Ambassador to Portugal in the sixteenth century, sent some tobacco to France, never realising that one of the weed's constituents, in which he was only mildly interested, would be named after him.

Sandwich John Montagu, fourth Earl of Sandwich, once spent twenty-four hours at the gaming tables, subsisting on slices of meat placed between two slices of bread. Food prepared in this way was named after him.

Saxophone Antoine Joseph Sax, of Dinant, Belguim, invented a number of musical instruments, all of which he called saxophones. Originally used in military bands, the 'sax' became popular about 1914–18 when it was featured in jazz bands.

Silhouette Like Guillotin and the guillotine Etienne de Silhouette had nothing to do with the shadow-outline pictures that bear his name. He was the French Minister of Finance in 1759 and his passion for economy made his name a byword for anything plain and cheap.

Wallop This word derives from the name of Sir John Wallop, who was ordered by King Henry VIII to invade France. He is said to have destroyed many towns and villages and 'walloped the foe to his heart's content'.

Wellington This kind of high boot takes its name from the Duke of Wellington who wore such boots during the Napoleonic Wars. In his day these boots were worn with trousers over them, but the name survives and is now applied to rubber boots reaching up to the knees.

12 Records

No, not gramophone records, you dum dum. They're under Entertainment (pop music section) aren't they? Do I have to tell you everything? Surely you can find your way round this book by now. Anyway, what we now present are some various record-breaking achievements, starting with some rather daft ones. . . .

Records: oddest

Roy Castle, who presents BBC-TV's *The Record Breakers*, a show which is based on listings in the *Guinness Book of Records*, has chosen what he considers the oddest British ones he has come across so far. The comments after each record are Mr Castle's very own remarks. . . .

1 *Demolition*
On 4 June 1972, Phil Milner, who is a karate third dan, led fifteen members of the International Judo Association in the demolition of a six-roomed Victorian house at Idle, Bradford,

using only their heads, feet and bare hands. It took them just six hours.

'Victorian cement takes years to dry. Don't use it.'

2 *Stair-climbing*

Bill Stevenson, a member of the Houses of Parliament Maintenance and Engineering Division, has had to climb 334 of the 364 steps of St Stephen's Tower 2829 times in ten years. It is equivalent to climbing Mount Everest over seventeen times.

'Too mean to buy oxygen equipment – warm clothing . . . and a watch.'

3 *Fishing contest*

At Buckenham, Ferry, Norfolk, on 9 January 1977, Peter Christian took part in a fishing contest with 107 other competitors. He won by catching a fish that weighed one-sixteenth of an ounce.

'Ate it for tea – "off the bone".'

4 *Football bookings*

On 3 November 1969, in a local cup match between Tongham Youth Club and Horley, the referee booked all twenty-two players and one of the linesmen. Tongham won 2–0, and the match was described by one of the players as 'a good, hard game'.

'The replay is at Wormwood Scrubs in three years. Two years with good conduct.'

In another football match at Waltham Abbey on 23 December 1973, M. J. Woodhams, refereeing a Gancia Cup match, sent off the entire Juventus-Cross team together with some of their officials.

'They lost 200 nil – all scored in the second half.'

5 *Slow pigeon*

On 29 September 1974, a pigeon named Blue Clip belonging to Harold Hart arrived home in its loft in Leigh, Greater Manchester. It had been released in Rennes, France over seven years earlier. The distance of 370 miles meant the pigeon had an average speed of 0·00589 mph which is slower than the world's fastest snail.

'It has also visited more unknown towns than any other pigeon.'

6 Singing

At a choral competition in Wales, only one choir entered, and did not even win the first prize. The judges said that as a punishment for arriving forty-five minutes late, they would only place them second.

'First prize was awarded to a tone-deaf busload who couldn't sing but arrived on time.'

7 Bus service

In 1976, it was reported that buses on the Hanley-Bagnoll route in Staffordshire would not stop for passengers. After complaints, Councillor Arthur Cholorton stated that if those buses stopped to pick up passengers, they would disrupt the timetable.

'Still applies. The service is in the red.'

8 TV commercial

Comedienne Pat Coombes had twenty-eight takes whilst making a commercial for a breakfast cereal. Each time she forgot the same thing – the name of the product. The commercial was never finished and the product was taken off the market.

'No one could remember it.'

9 Football crowd

On 7 May 1921, Leicester City played Stockport County at Manchester United's ground. Only thirteen people turned up to watch it.

'There was polo at Hurley.'

10 Misprints

On 22 August 1978, on page 19 of *The Times*, there were 97 misprints in $5\frac{1}{2}$ single column inches. The passage was about 'Pop' (Pope) Paul VI.

'It wsa mist unterusting reedink.'

Record speeds in sport

Some interesting speeds supplied by George Mell. Thank you, Mr Mell.

1 Howard Hill, American **archer**, claimed that arrows from his bow often travelled at   322 km/h (200 mph)

2 American **golfer** Wood Platt made a timed drive from the tee at   290 km/h (180 mph)

3 William T. Tilden, American **tennis** ace, was timed serving at   263 km/h (163·6 mph)

4 **Cycling** behind a car fitted with a wind shield in Utah, USA, in 1973, Dr Allan V. Abbott reached a speed of   226 km/h (140·5 mph)

5 Joe Louis, ex-heavyweight **boxing** champion, delivered punches travelling only 25 cm (10in) at   204 km/h (127 mph)

6 Steve McKinney, **skiing** in a 500-metre race in Chile in 1978 travelled at   200 km/h (124·4 mph)

7 In **ice hockey** the puck has been timed travelling at   190·3 km/h (118·3 mph)

8 Jeff Thomson, Australian **cricket** player, has been timed bowling at   147·6 km/h (91·8 mph)

9 In 1975 the Swiss Poldi Berchtold set a record speed for a **bobsleigh** on the Cresta Run of   82 km/h (50·9 mph)

10 The record speed for a **racehorse** was set by Big Racket over 402 metres (quarter mile) in Mexico in 1945   70 km/h (43·26 mph)

11 The record **ice skating** speed
was set by the Russian Evgeni
Kulikov in 1975   48·6 km/h (30·22 mph)
12 In 1963 Robert Lee Hayes of the
USA **ran** 91·4m (100 yd) at   43·5 km/h (27 mph)
13 In Sicily in 1963 Giuseppe
Cantarella **roller skated** at   41·4 km/h (25·78 mph)
14 A **billiards** ball has been timed
travelling at   35·4 km/h (22 mph)
15 In 1977 the world's fastest
swimmer, Joe Bottom of the
USA, covered 45·7m (50yd) at   8·35 km/h (5·19 mph)

The world's fastest cars

1 (rocket-engined) *The Blue Flame*, driven by Gary Gabelich
of the USA on Bonneville Salt Flats, Utah, USA on 23
October 1970 at 1016·086 km/h (631·367 mph)
2 (jet-engined) *Spirit of America*, driven by Norman Craig
Breedlove of the USA on Bonneville Salt Flats, Utah,
USA on 15 November 1965 at 988·129 km/h (613·995
mph)
3 (wheel-driven) *Bluebird*, driven by Donald Malcolm Camp-
bell of Great Britain on salt flats at Lake Eyre, Southern
Australia on 17 July 1964 at 690·909 km/h (429·311 mph)
4 (piston-engined) *Goldenrod*, driven by Robert Sherman
Summers of the USA on Bonneville Salt Flats, Utah,
USA on 12 November 1965 at 673·516 km/h (418·504
mph)
5 (racing car) Porsche 917/30 Can-Am, driven by Mark
Donohue of the USA on the Paul Ricard circuit near
Toulouse, France in August 1973 at 413·6 km/h (257
mph)
6 (diesel-engined) 3-litre Mercedes C 111/3, driven on the
Nardo circuit, southern Italy between 5 and 15 October
1978 at 327·3 km/h (203·3 mph)
7 (road car) Ferrari BB Berlinetta Boxer 262·3 km/h (163
mph)

Railway records

The longest bridge isn't likely to get any longer, or the highest station to rise any more, at least not in the next few years, but the speed records will soon be increasing, thanks to the Advanced Passenger Train. The APT is electric, with the power car in the middle, and has a tilt mechanism which can take it round corners in safety and comfort at great speed – 40% faster than normal trains.

The best of British Rail

Longest bridge: TAY BRIDGE 3·9 km (2 miles 365 yds)

Bridge with longest span: FORTH BRIDGE two spans, each 520 m (1710 ft)

Highest railway bridge: BALLOCHMYLE VIADUCT (on the line between Glasgow and Carlisle) 50 m (164 ft) above river bed

Longest tunnel: SEVERN TUNNEL 7 km (4 miles 628 yds)

Longest straight: BETWEEN SELBY AND HULL 29 km (18 miles)

Highest altitude: DRUIMUACHDAR 450 m (1484 ft) above sea level

Lowest point: SEVERN TUNNEL 44 m (144 ft) below sea level

Steepest mainline gradient: LICKEY INCLINE 1 in 37·7 (nearly 3·2 km/2 miles)

Highest station: CORROUR, Inverness-shire 404 m (1327 ft)

Station with most platforms: WATERLOO 21 platforms

Station with longest platform: COLCHESTER 585 m (1920 ft)

Busiest junction: CLAPHAM JUNCTION over 2000 trains every weekday

Highest speeds: ADVANCED PASSENGER TRAIN 257·5 km/h (160 mph) (20 December 1979) HIGH SPEED TRAIN 235 km/h (143 mph) (12 June 1973)

Fastest scheduled passenger train: PADDINGTON – BRISTOL PARKWAY, 120 km (112 miles) Inter-City 125 Average 165·76 km/h (103·15 mph)

Fastest-ever train journey: PADDINGTON-CHIPPENHAM Inter-City 125 Average 178·6 km/h (111·7 mph) over 151 km (94 miles) (10 April 1979, possible world record)

Longest train journey: THE CLANSMAN – Euston-Inverness via
Birmingham 914 km (586 miles)
Heaviest train: carries iron ore, PORT TALBOT-LLANWERN 3000
tonnes gross
Only BR steam route: VALE OF RHEIDOL LINE, Aberystwyth-
Devil's Bridge 60 cm gauge: 19 km (11¾ miles)

Progressive rail speed records since 1900

162·5 km/h (101·0 mph) Siemens und Halske Electric near
Berlin, 1901
193·1 km/h (120·0 mph) Savannah, Florida and Western Railway mail train No. 111, Screven to Satilla, Florida, USA, 1
March 1901
200·99 km/h (124·89 mph) Siemens und Halske Electric,
Mariensfeld-Zossen, near Berlin, 6 October 1903
206·69 km/h (128·43 mph) Siemens und Halske Electric,
Mariensfeld-Zossen, near Berlin, 23 October 1903
210·19 km/h (130·61 mph) Siemens und Halske Electric,
Mariensfeld-Zossen, near Berlin, 27 October 1903
230·1 km/h (143·0 mph) Kruckenberg (propeller-driven),
Karstadt-Cergenthin, Germany, 21 June 1931
242·9 km/h (150·9 mph) Co-Co SNCF No. 7121 Electric,
Dijon-Beaune, France, 21 February 1954
330·9 km/h (205·6 mph) Co-Co SNCF No. 7107 Electric,
Facture-Morcenx, France, 28 March 1955
330·9 km/h (205·6 mph) Bo-Bo SNCF No. 9004 Electric,
Facture-Morcenx, France, 29 March 1955
378 km/h (235 mph) *L'Aerotrain* (jet aero engines), Gometz
le Châtel-Limours, France, 4 December 1967
376·9 km/h (234·2 mph) linear induction motor research
vehicle, Pueblo, Colorado, USA, 28 March 1974

Oldest railways

1 Great Britain 1825
2 Spain 1828

3 USA 1830
4 France 1832
5 Ireland 1834
6 Germany 1835
7 Canada 1836
8 USSR 1837
9 Czechoslovakia and Italy 1839
10 Poland 1842

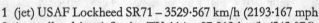

The word's fastest aircraft

1 (jet) USAF Lockheed SR71 – 3529·567 km/h (2193·167 mph

2 (propeller-driven) Soviet TU-114 – 87·212 km/h (545·076)
   mph)

3 (piston-engined) Hawker *Sea Fury* – 836 km/h (520 mph)

4 (biplane) Italian Fiat CR42B – 520 km/h (323 mph)

5 (bomber) French Dassault *Mirage IV* – 2333 km/h (1450
   mph)

6 (airliner) BAC/Aerospatiale *Concorde* – 1876·54 km/h
   (1166·031 mph)

13 Home Facts

Back to some simple factual lists, with a world-wide view.
They're mostly about the home, except the ones which are not
about the home . . . .

Telephones

Telephones in use per 1000 population

1	USA	677
2	Denmark	428
3	Luxembourg	397
4	UK	366
5	Japan	356
6	Netherlands	344
7	W. Germany	302
8	Belgium	272
9	Italy	246
10	France	236

11 Irish Republic 127
12 USSR 62

Televisions

Television receivers in use per 1000 population

EEC statistics, 1975

1	USA	571
2	UK	315
3	Denmark	308
4	W. Germany	305
5	Netherlands	259
6	Luxembourg	257
7	Belgium	252
8	France	235
9	Japan	233
10	Italy	213
11	USSR	208
12	Irish Republic	178

Cars

In Britain

These figures of motor vehicles in the UK are based on the number of vehicle licences issued each year, from Department of Transport figures.

type of vehicle	*thousands*
Private cars & private vans	14 417
Motorcycles, scooters & mopeds	1211
Goods	1743
Agricultural tractors	408
Other vehicles	311
Public transport vehicles	111
All vehicles	18 201

Round the world

The USA has the highest number of cars per 1000 of the population, but Japan has the highest increase – from one per 1000 in 1953 to 180 per 1000 in 1977. In 1977, six out of ten families in Great Britain had regular use of a car, and more than one family in ten had two or more cars. In Scotland, however, fifty-four per cent of families did not have a car, and only seven per cent had two or more cars.

Car ownership: international comparison

| | number of cars per 1000 population | | | | | |
	1953	1961	1966	1971	1976	1977
USA	288	345	400	427	510	530
Sweden	60	175	241	291	351	346
W. Germany	22	95	179	247	308	326
France	47	135	210	261	300	315
Italy	13	50	125	209	284	290
Netherlands	18	55	121	212	269	283
UK	57	116	181	225	253	260
Japan	1	8	28	102	160	180

The UK comes surprisingly low on the list.

Electricity

In an all-electric house, the average British family of four consumes almost 19 000 units of electricity a year. This is where it goes.

Electricity consumed
– units per year per household

Central heating	10 000
Heating water	3500
Cooker	2000
Dishwasher	850

Washing machine	270
Deep freeze	900
Colour TV	500
Fridge	325
Electric kettle	250
Lighting	200
Electric iron	75
Vacuum cleaner	30
Toaster	20
	18 920

Water

In the average British household (of four people) each person uses over 12 000 gallons of water a year. This is where it goes.

	gallons per year per person
Lavatory	4560
Washing and bathing	4560
Dishwasher and cleaning	1280
Laundry	1280
Garden	550
Drinking and cooking	365
Car washing	182
	12 777

14 Last Words

A few well-chosen epitaphs, to finish off any book, or any life. . . .

He rocked the boat,
Did Ezra Shank.
These bubbles o
        o
          o
              o mark
Where Ezra sank.

Here lies the body of Ann Mann
Who lived an old woman
And died an old Mann.

'Er as was 'as gone from we,
Us as is'll go ter she.

Epitaph on a dentist

Stranger! Approach this spot with gravity.
John Brown is filling his last cavity.

On Dr Chard

Here lies the corpse of Doctor Chard,
Who filled half of this churchyard.

Elizabeth Ireland, died 1779

> Here I lie, at the chancel door,
> Here I lie because I'm poor.
> The farther in, the more you pay;
> Here lie I as warm as they.
>   Ashburton, Devon

Poor little Johnny
We'll never see him more –
For what he thought was H_2O
was H_2SO_4.

The wife's epitaph

To follow you I'm not content.
How do I know which way you went?

Here lyes the bodeys of George Young
and Isabel Guthrie, and all their posterity
for fifty years backwards. November 1757.
                    Montrose, Angus

He passed the bobby without any fuss,
And he passed the cart of hay,
He tried to pass a swerving bus,
And then he passed away.

Here lies the body of Michael Shay
Who died maintaining his right of way.
His case was clear and his will was strong –
But he's as dead as if he'd been wrong.

Here lies the body of Elizabeth White;
She signalled left, but turned to the right.

Beyond these gates
Tom Green's at rest;
He took off his plates
But hadn't passed his test.

Beneath this stone, a lump of clay,
Lies Uncle Peter Dan'els,
Who, early in the month of May,
Took off his winter flannels.

Erected to the memory of John MacFarlane, drowned in the
waters of the Leith by a few affectionate friends.

On Mary Ann Lowder

Here lies the body of Mary Ann Lowder,
She burst while drinking a seidlitz powder.
Called from this world to her heavenly rest,
She should have waited till it effervesced.

Cheltenham waters

Here lie I and my four daughters
Killed by drinking Cheltenham waters.
Had we but stuck to Epsom salts,
   We wouldn't have been in these here vaults.

On Leslie Moore

Here lies what's left
Of Leslie Moore –
   No Les
   No more.
            Unknown

On Hunter Davies

He did some lists
And now he's listless
          Very unknown

More Beaver Books

We hope you have enjoyed this Beaver Book. Here are some of the other titles:

The Beaver Book of Crazy Inventions A Beaver original. From the snore-stop to the ninety-degree rifle, a collection of absurd inventions (all of which were patented), to amuse and amaze you. The inventions are described by Joseph Brundene and illustrations are reproduced from the original patents, with cartoons by David Mostyn

The Beaver Book of Fishing A Beaver original. Everything the young angler needs to know about fishing in rivers, reservoirs and the sea, with detailed information about techniques, tackle and bait. By Alan Wrangles; illustrated by John Reynolds

Maggie Four lively books about Maggie McKinley, the irrepressible Glasgow teenager who determines to live her own life despite problems with her family and her over-enthusiastic boyfriend, James. The books are called *The Clearance*, *The Resettling*, *The Pilgrimage* and *The Reunion*; written by Joan Lingard, they were the basis for the TV series *Maggie* and will be thoroughly enjoyed by all older readers

These and many other Beavers are available from your local bookshop or newsagent, or can be ordered direct from: Hamlyn Paperback Cash Sales, PO Box 11, Falmouth, Cornwall TR10 9EN. Send a cheque or postal order, made payable to the Hamlyn Publishing Group, for the price of the book plus postage at the following rates:
UK: 40p for the first book, 18p for the second book, and 13p for each additional book ordered to a maximum charge of £1·49;
BFPO and Eire: 40p for the first book, 18p for the second book, plus 13p per copy for the next 7 books and thereafter 7p per book;
OVERSEAS: 60p for the first book and 18p for each extra book.

New Beavers are published every month and if you would like the *Beaver Bulletin*, a newsletter which tells you about new books and gives a complete list of titles and prices, send a large stamped addressed envelope to:

Beaver Bulletin
Hamlyn Paperbacks
Banda House
Cambridge Grove
London W6 0LE

203948